THE DESKTOP BUSINESS INTELLIGENCE SOURCEBOOK

A Comprehensive Guidebook For The Information Age

First Edition

Kent R. Frantzve

Hyde Park Marketing Group

Please note . . .

While every effort has been made to ensure that the listing of sources is both current and complete, some sources may not be included. Other sources, which have been included, may have subsequently decided to terminate publication, be withdrawn, or otherwise not be readily available for reference. We assume no responsibility for errors or omissions and reserve the right to include or eliminate listings and otherwise edit the lists based on our judgement as to what is useful to our readers.

Original Executive Edition

First Printing: November 1992

Published by:
Hyde Park Marketing Group
Post Office Box 8804
Cincinnati, Ohio 45208

Copies of this book may be ordered directly from the publisher for $16.95 plus $3.00 for postage and handling (Ohio residents please add 6% state sales tax). For terms on ordering volume quantities, please write the publisher.

Library of Congress Catalog Card Number: 91-72603
ISBN: 1-880186-00-4

Printed in the United States of America.

TABLE OF CONTENTS

FOREWORD

During the past 30 years, more information has been created than in the previous 30 centuries. Experts estimate that the amount of new information and knowledge being generated literally doubles every five years. It is little wonder that the ability to find, analyze and use specific information offers a critical advantage to any business professional.

A short time ago, I had to put together a new venture business plan without the usual "corporate" resources at my disposal. I spent many long hours at my local university and public library digging for data. My biggest frustration was trying to locate the exact information I needed to support the details of the plan. I had no one resource to turn to that would allow me to sift through the many thousands of books, periodicals and other publications that were scattered in front of me. Consequently, I spent a great deal of time and effort screening many information resources to come up with my supporting facts, figures, charts and quotations for the business plan.

Throughout all of this, I did have an advantage over the average executive or entrepreneur. I was able to rely on my twenty year career in marketing and marketing research for understanding and guidance through the information maze. Most of the sourcebooks I looked at for help contained too much verbiage, and were incomplete or outdated.

Preparing business plans, research papers, business cases, market assessments and other business-related projects require correct and timely information. Knowing exactly where to look for this information is critical. Since there is so little on the market to turn to for help, we decided to develop just such a guidebook.

The Desktop Business Intelligence Sourcebook was designed to provide general research guidance to anyone seeking business information. Whether you are an entrepreneur, senior executive, marketing researcher, business planner or business student, you will benefit from this book. It is intended to be a single-source guide to the best business data and information resources currently available. By using this book beforehand, you will save a tremendous amount of time and effort in securing the right information for your project. Whatever the question or task, this book simply points you in the right direction as to where you can find the right answers or data.

From a quality and usefulness perspective, our guess is that this book will not only meet, but exceed your referencing expectations and that you will want to purchase an extra copy for a friend or colleague. We invite you to write us with your comments and suggestions concerning *The Desktop Business Intelligence Sourcebook.*

Kent R. Frantzve
President

HYDE PARK MARKETING GROUP
Post Office Box 8804
Cincinnati, Ohio 45208

ACKNOWLEDGMENTS

The author wishes to acknowledge and thank the Business Reference Department at the Public Library of Cincinnati and Hamilton County, the University of Cincinnati Langsam Library, and the New York Public Library for their resources and help in compiling the materials for this book.

Additional thanks go to Tom Sant of *Sant and Associates*, Ken Schonberg of *Schonberg and Associates*, John Graham of the *Cincinnati Public Library*, Paul Slaggert of the *University of Cincinnati*, Mike Dean of *Matrixx Marketing,* Tom Hayes of *Xavier University* and Dick Vorndran for reviewing the content, layout and design of the book.

And of course, a tremendous amount of appreciation goes to my wife, Lori, without whose support this work would not have been possible.

"Information, rather than oil or steel, is likely to become the most precious commercial resource, and the company that can gather, evaluate, and synthesize information ahead of its rivals will have a competitive advantage."

- The New York Times
May 13, 1990

INTRODUCTION

It has been said that information is the life-blood of our modern American society. We make business and personal decisions every day based largely upon the information and data that is available to us. What we do and what we accomplish is governed by what we learn from information sources. Access to information is truly a necessary tool in our everyday lives.

Each month more and more business related data and information is collected, stored, published and otherwise made available by a variety of reporting sources. This wealth of valuable business information is available to all of us--if we know where to look for it. To find the most relevant and current information applicable to your specific needs, it is oftentimes necessary to search through many sources, some of which are not easily accessible. This process can be very time consuming and expensive, unless you know exactly what information is available and where it can be found.

The purpose of this book is to provide general research guidance to all those who seek business related data and information, regardless of their skill level. Preparing business plans, research papers, market assessments and other business projects require correct and timely information. Knowing exactly where to go for this information is critical. Whether you are an entrepreneur, student, marketing researcher, business planner, senior or junior executive, you will benefit from this book. It is intended to be a single source reference guide to the best business data and information resources currently available. By using this guide beforehand, you will save a tremendous amount of time and effort in securing the right information for your project. Whatever the question or task, this volume will point you in the right direction as to where you can find the necessary answers or data. Your next steps involve physically getting the information. In this regard, your public library is your greatest information resource. Most comprehensive reference works are far too expensive to be practical purchases for an individual, however your local library has many of them on its shelves. Literally hundreds of reference sources and services are available to assist you in completing any project, large or small.

It should be noted that the old, familiar card catalog has become almost obsolete due to the onrush of new information technology. More and more, they are being replaced by computer-based catalogs. The new electronic library catalogs contain millions of entries that are more up-to-date, better organized, and accessed far more easily than the traditional card catalogs ever could be. The new cataloging systems will also tell you which nearby library has the reference materials you seek.

You should view this book as a desk-reference companion to your other information source books, whether they are as comprehensive as Dun's total business reference library, or as simple as Webster's Dictionary and the Yellow Pages. It is our hope that this book will be a welcome addition to your own office or home library, and be of help to you in your daily business planning and decision-making.

LIBRARY SOURCES

There are five types of business libraries wherein relevant information can be found:

1. City or county public library
2. College or university library
3. Corporate or private organization library
4. Professional association library
5. Governmental library

No one library has all the available reference materials, however your chances of finding the information you need are much greater at a large urban library or a college library that supports a business program. The following selection of business libraries are among the best in the country.

Leading Business Libraries

American Management Association Library
135 West 50th Street
New York, NY 10020
212/903-8182

Offers many services, however open to members only. Covers management, personnel, marketing, finance, production, and international operations. Has over 10,000 books and 175 file drawers of articles, pamphlets, and company documents.

Boston Public Library
(Kirsten Business Branch)
20 City Hall Avenue
Boston, MA 02108
617/523-0860

Covers all aspects of business related subjects including accounting, management and finance. Special collection has annual reports of foreign companies and many foreign telephone directories. Also a U.S. Government Documents depository; publishes a monthly newsletter.

Chicago Public Library
(Business/Science/Technology Division)
400 North Franklin Street
Chicago, IL 60611
312/269-2814

Library covers all business topics including marketing, small business, investments, and personnel, as well as related scientific topics: technology, patents, medicine, physics and biology, and computer science. Has over 60,000 volumes, 50 drawers of corporate annual reports, and SEC reports. Includes special collections of complete U.S. and British patents, gazettes, domestic and foreign auto manuals, career information, electrical and computer schematics, and industrial, corporate and product directories.

Columbia University
(Thomas J. Watson Library of Business and Economics)
130 Uris Hall
New York, NY 10027
212/280-4000

Covers all business related subjects including banking and finance, management, marketing, labor relations, law, agriculture, and transportation. Has over 350,000 volumes.

Harvard University
(Harvard Business School, Baker Library)
Soldiers Field Road
Boston, MA 02163
617/495-6044

Holds over 540,000 volumes on all aspects of business management and economics. Special collections include corporate reports, manuscripts, and archives.

Massachusetts Institute of Technology
(Dewey Library)
Hermann Building, E53-100
Cambridge, MA 02139
617/253-5677

Covers economics, finance, management, psychology, sociology, law, and political science. Has over 375,000 volumes, including 125,000 pamphlets, 25,000 technical reports, and over 5,000 M.I.T. theses. Includes special collections on industrial relations, corporate financial reports, and United Nations documents.

New York Public Library
(Economic and Public Affairs Division)
Fifth Avenue and 42nd Street, Room 228
New York, NY 10018
212/930-0750

Covers business related subjects such as marketing, labor banking and insurance; also covers government publications and demographics, and has census and other statistical information. Holds over 1.5 million books.

Seattle Public Library
(Business and Science Department)
1000 Fourth Avenue
Seattle, WA 98104
206/386-4655

Covers regional business and economics, skilled trades, and investments. Has over 250,000 books, as well as other research materials.

Stanford University
(J. Hugh Jackson Library)
Graduate School of Business
Stanford, CA 94305-5016
415/723-2161

Special collections emphasize economics and business of the Pacific Northwest. Has more than 365,000 volumes.

University of Alabama
(Business Library)
Box 870266
Tuscaloosa, AL 35487-0266
205/348-6096

Covers all aspects of business including accounting, banking and finance, economics, marketing, real estate, insurance, business law, and statistics. Has a sizable collections of corporate annual reports.

University of California, Los Angeles (UCLA)
(John E. Anderson Graduate School of Management Library)
Los Angeles, CA 90024-1460
213/825-3138

Has material on all fields of business and management, including accounting, finance, investments, labor relations, marketing, arts management, and urban land economics.

University of Chicago
(Joseph Regenstein Library, Business and Economics)
1100 East 57th Street
Chicago, IL 60637
312/702-8716

Covers business economics, management, finance, and accounting. Holds over 375,000 volumes.

University of Michigan
(Kresge Business Administration Library)
School of Business Administration
Tappan and Monroe Streets
Ann Arbor, MI 48109-1234
313/764-7356

Covers accounting, finance, marketing, management, banking and related subjects. Holds over 208,000 books, government documents, corporate financial reports, other reports, and supporting materials.

University of Pennsylvania
(Lippincott Library of the Wharton School)
3420 Walnut Street
Philadelphia, PA 19104-6207
215/898-5924

Covers business, management, organizational behavior, finance, economics, and marketing. Has over 65,000 books, bound periodical volumes, corporate annual reports, and 10K reports.

HOW TO USE THIS BOOK

The Desktop Business Intelligence Sourcebook is designed to function as a workbook, as well as a continuing reference. To locate information sources on a specific subject, start with the Table of Contents. The material in this book is generally arranged by type of information source rather than by topic so that the business executive, marketer, researcher or student can locate specific resources easily, while at the same time, gain an understanding of the kinds of information most likely to be available in each of the broad source categories. All entries are listed alphabetically within each category. Next, consult the Index, which will pinpoint the names of references on specific topics. Finally, if you are short on time and have no idea where to begin your information search, turn to the "**Quick Reference Guide to Business Information Power Sources,**" found toward the end of this book. These sources are the most productive and easiest to use for finding information on almost any business topic. For your convenience, project worksheets have been provided at the back of this book to help you organize and begin your own information searches.

Individual references in this book have been objectively selected on the basis of their general usefulness. No attempt has been made to produce an exhaustive bibliography. In fact, no information guide, regardless of how extensive and exhaustive, can even come close to listing all the sources and materials available to the information searcher. New resources appear each day. However, every effort has been made to include the most current business information sources available.

"Knowledge is of two kinds. We know a subject ourselves, or we know where we can find information upon it."

- Samuel Johnson, 1775

GENERAL BUSINESS INFORMATION GUIDES

The following source books are very general and broad in nature, but will be helpful to anyone initiating a basic library search on a business or business-related topic.

Business Information: Applications and Sources
By: *Van Mayros and D. Michael Werner (Chilton);* 1983.
Lists more than 3800 information sources, including 400 on-line data bases. Other sources are periodicals, information services and brokers, government agencies and publications, general reference works, and a variety of materials dealing with information applications.

Business Information: How to Find It, How to Use It
By: *Michael R. Lavin (Oryx Press);* 1992.
Helps one locate specific sources of business data, also serves as a handbook to help understand the various techniques of researching information. Has short, in-depth descriptions of major business publications and databases with tips on how to use them effectively.

Business Information Sources
By: *Lorna Daniells (University of California Press);* 1985.
A comprehensive source book on business information; describes sources for various disciplines, industries and products.

Business Researcher's Handbook: The Comprehensive Guide for Business Professionals
By: *Washington Researchers, Ltd.;* 1983.
An excellent research tool covering all facets of business. Easy to understand; well indexed.

Data Sources for Business and Market Analysis
By: *Nathalie Frank and John Ganly (Scarecrow Press);* 1983.
An annotated guide to business data sources. Very useful to the marketing researcher. Information is arranged by type of source rather than by topic.

Directories in Print
By: *Gale Research, Inc.;* 1992.
An annotated guide in two volumes to over 14,000

directories published world-wide; includes all professional, business and industrial directories, plus other areas. A detailed Subject Index contains over 3,500 subject headings.

Directory of International Sources of Business Information

By: *Sarah Ball (Pitman Publishing Ltd. London);* 1989.

This work is targeted toward the field of international investment and focuses on companies, markets, finance, securities and economics in the U.S.A., Canada, Europe and the Far East. Entries organized by: country data sources, industry data sources, online databases--background and descriptions.

Encyclopedia of Business Information Sources

By: *Gale Research, Inc.;* 1988.

A detailed listing of 1,000 critical subjects of interest to management personnel; contains a list of source books, periodicals, on-line data bases, organizations, directories, handbooks, bibliographies, and other information sources.

Guide to American Directories

By: *B. Kline Publications, Inc.;* 1990.

A general guide to over 1,500 major business directories of the U.S., covering all industrial, professional and trade categories. It is designed to aid each type of business and industry in locating new markets for its products through dependable mailing list sources, and to assist other business researchers find current and reliable information sources.

Handbook of Business Information: A Guide for Librarians, Students and Researchers

By: *Diane Wheeler Strauss (Libraries Unlimited, Inc.);* 1988.

A 500-page reference book organized into the following sections: basic business reference sources, directories, periodicals and newspapers, looseleaf services, government information services, statistics, vertical file collections, electronic business information, marketing, accounting and taxation, money, credit and banking, investments, stocks, bonds and other fixed income securities, mutual funds and investment companies, futures and options, insurance and real estate.

How to Find Information About Companies: The Corporate Intelligence Source Book

By: *Washington Researchers;* 1983.

A guide to information on corporations available from government agencies and computer data bases. The book is designed for the serious researcher seeking information not readily available in published sources.

Information Sources in Management and Business

By: *K.O.C. Vernon (Butterworth's Guides to Information Sources);* 1984.

This source book is British in origin and spans both U.S. and European literature of management. (The British counterpart to Daniells' "*Business Information Sources.*")

Sources of World Financial and Banking Information

By: *G.R. Dicks (Greenwood Press);* 1981.

Organized into three sections. Section I lists 5,000 sources of data in banking and finance alphabetically by country. Section II gives additional details on the sources listed in Section I. Section III is a classification of the material according to a seven-part indexing system by subject.

The Basic Business Library: Core Resources

By: *Bernard S. Schlesinger (Oryx Press);* 1989.

A librarian's resource that reveals an abundance of business information materials. This was originally developed as a list of economical start-up sources for small and medium-sized libraries.

The New York Public Library Book of How and Where to Look It Up

By: *Sherwood Harris (Stonesong Press/Prentice Hall);* 1991.

Designed for general consumers and professionals alike, the volume is divided into six major categories: Reference Books, Telephone Sources, Government Sources, Picture Sources, Special Collections, and Electronic Databases. Each section lists the primary locations of information in each category and is organized by subject from A to Z, with sources listed alphabetically under each subject heading.

Where to Find Business Information
By: *David M. Brownstone (John Wiley & Sons);* 1982.
A domestic and international subject guide covering all areas of business sources. Includes over 5,000 sources and includes a publisher's index.

"Even if you know you have an information problem and you are able to get the information you need, you must still be able to interpret the information accurately and apply it to your situation. Having the right information is not the same as knowing what to do with it."

- John H. Everett,
Information For Sale

INDEX AND ABSTRACT SERVICES

PRINTED (Hard Copy)

The following information sources are available in printed form, often referred to as "hard copy." Updates are usually issued on a monthly or quarterly basis.

Accountant's Index
By: *American Institute of Certified Public Accountants.*
A comprehensive index to books, pamphlets and articles on finance and accounting. Listings are arranged by author, title and subject. The source of each article or publication is given. A publishers directory at the end of the volume shows where each publication can be obtained. Updates are quarterly.

Applied Science and Technology Index
By: *H.W. Wilson Company.*
A subject index to over 200 selected journals in the fields of aeronautics, automation, chemistry, construction, electricity, electronics, engineering, geology and metallurgy, industrial and mechanical arts, machinery, physics, transportation and related subjects. Updated monthly.

Banking Literature Index
By: *American Bankers Association.*
A subject index to current periodical articles on banking trends, topics, issues and operations. The focus of the index is toward practical banking management. Published monthly with an annual cumulation.

Books in Print
By: *R.R. Bowker.*
A publication listing all in-print and forthcoming titles from over 35,000 publishers. Contains books covering all subjects, provided they are published or distributed in the U.S. and are available to the trade or general public for purchase. Published annually.

Business Index

By: *NewsBank, Inc.*

NewsBank is a reference service providing company, industry and product news from more than 500 U.S. cities. This is a microfiche index to approximately 650 journals and major financial newspapers (with only a three to four week lag). Articles are grouped by industry. The monthly index cumulates the previous months.

Business International Index

By: *Business International Corporation (Praeger).*

This is a quarterly index to the publications of Business International Corporation. References on countries and subject terms are listed alphabetically in the first section of the index. Company references are indexed in a separate section following the terms and country index. Published annually.

Business Periodicals Index

By: *H.W. Wilson Company.*

Indexes approximately 300 periodicals. Entries are listed alphabetically according to subject title. This classical index to business periodicals is still an excellent source of business information (lag time is six to eight weeks). It can be used in conjunction with the Business Index. Published monthly.

Computer Literature Index

By: *Applied Computer Research.*

This index focuses on the user end of the computer profession. It is application oriented and therefore a source of information for the business researcher. It is published four times a year, with an annual cumulation.

Conference Board Cumulative Index

By: *The Conference Board.*

Covers Conference Board publications in the fields of administration, business, economics, finance, personnel, marketing, international operations and public affairs. All publications are indexed according to subject. This annual index is cumulative and includes publications of the last five years plus selected reports from previous years.

Consumers Index to Product Evaluations and Information Sources

By: *Pierian Press.*

This is an index to journal articles about consumerism. The main focus is on product evaluations and tests. Issued annually with quarterly supplements.

Corporate & Industry Research Reports Index

By: *R.R. Bowker.*

Contains over 147,000 research reports on industries, companies and products prepared by leading analysts and economists from more than 100 major investment firms. Published annually.

Human Resources Abstracts

By: *Institute of Labor & Industrial Relations of the University of Michigan and Wayne State University.*

This is a quarterly abstracting service covering human, social and manpower areas. Entries are classified by broad subject categories. Published quarterly with an annual cumulative index by author and subject.

The Index and Abstract Directory

By: *EBSCO Publishing, Inc.*

An international guide to abstract services and publication coverage that also includes online services. Over 35,000 titles are arranged by subject, within subject, alphabetically by title. This is a highly technical and exhaustive reference work.

Index to U.S. Government Publications

By: *Infordata International.*

This work indexes more than 200 periodicals published by U.S. Government Agencies. It is published quarterly with annual cumulations.

Journal of Economic Literature

By: *American Economic Association.*

This source indexes major economic periodicals of prime interest to business and economic researchers. Each issue includes: an annotated list of new books, classified by subject; a subject index of articles in current periodicals; selected abstracts of the more significant articles, by subjects; and tables of contents for current economic journals. Critical book reviews are at the beginning of each issue. The Economic Literature Index is the online counterpart to this work. Updated quarterly.

Micro Computer Index
By: *Learned Information, Inc.*
This is a very comprehensive abstracts journal covering: computer software, computer applications, computer mathematics and computer electronics. It includes magazine articles, books, government publications, proceedings and dissertations. Issued monthly, with an annual cumulation of the subject index.

Monthly Catalog of U.S. Government Publications
By: *U.S. Government Printing Office.*
This is a current bibliography of publications issued by all branches of the government, including congressional publications. The main body of the text is arranged by the superintendent of documents classification system. Indexes by author, title, subject and series/report are provided. Issued monthly.

Personnel Management Abstracts
By: *Personnel Management Abstracts, Inc.*
Lists articles from a large number of academic and trade journals dealing with the management of people and organizational behavior. The index section is arranged by subject and author. A brief description of the article is given in the subject section. A number of articles are described in longer abstract form (about 250 words). Updated quarterly.

Predicasts F&S Index: United States
By: *Predicasts, Inc.*
This index is especially useful for corporate news. Subject matter includes: mergers and acquisitions, technological developments, analysis by security firms, labor relations, company earnings, government reports, etc. The index is arranged into two sections: SIC codes and company name. Updated weekly, with monthly, quarterly and annual indexes.

Predicasts F&S Index: Europe
By: *Predicasts, Inc.*

Covers company, product and industry information from financial publications, business newspapers, trade magazines, etc. covering all of Europe (excluding East European countries) Access is provided through three indexes: industries and products, countries, and companies. Updated monthly.

Predicasts F&S Index: International

By: *Predicasts, Inc.*

Covers similar publications as other F&S Indexes. The focus is international (excluding the U.S. and Europe). It is arranged in three parts: 1) by SIC code, 2) by countries, and 3) by company name. Issued monthly.

PROMT

By: *Predicasts, Inc.*

Predicast's Overview of Markets and Technology contains short article summaries covering industry news, food and agriculture, packaging and paper, polymers and polymer products, drugs and toiletries, chemicals, materials, electronics, machinery, transportation, consumer, health, safety, energy and environment. Articles are arranged by industry; has an alphabetical index at end of book. Updated weekly.

Psychological Abstracts

By: *American Psychological Association.*

Provides summaries of psychology and related literature. Covers the areas of general psychology, experimental psychology, social and applied psychology. Applied psychology is subdivided into: occupational attitudes and interests, personnel selection and training, personnel evaluation and performance, management and management training, organizational behavior and job satisfaction, human factors engineering, marketing and advertising. Updated monthly.

Public Affairs Information Service (PAIS)

By: *H.W. Wilson Company.*

PAIS lists, by subject, all current books, pamphlets, selected periodical articles, government documents and other useful library materials in economic and public affairs. Emphasis is placed on factual and statistical information. Updated quarterly.

Reader's Guide to Periodical Literature

By: *H.W. Wilson Company.*

Indexes articles in over 200 popular magazines such as Newsweek, Time, Sports Illustrated, Health, Ms., and Popular Science. Since the work references general interest publications, descriptions of technical matters are clearly defined and explained. Supplements are issued monthly.

Selected Rand Abstracts

By: *Rand Corporation.*

A subject index to Rand Corporation Books, reports and papers. All entries are abstracted. Updated quarterly.

Small Business Start-Up Index

By: *Gale Research, Inc.*

A guide to small business literature, broadly defined to include audio and video cassettes and a wide range of publications. A companion to Gale's Small Business Sourcebook, this index covers only topics relating to small businesses. Issued three times a year.

The Standard Periodical Directory

By: *Oxbridge Publishing Company.*

Provides data on more than 75,000 periodicals in the U.S. and Canada. Covers consumer magazines, directories, newspapers, newsletters, trade journals, yearbooks, association publications, an online service directory, and more. Published annually.

The Wall Street Journal Index (Including Barron's)

By: *Dow Jones, Inc.*

A very current index of the Wall Street Journal. Each issue is divided into two sections: 1) corporate news and 2) general news. Issued monthly; annual cumulations.

ELECTRONIC (Online and CD-ROM)

Many of the indexing and abstracting services are available online or on CD-ROM (Compact-Disk Read Only Memory) equipment at major university and public libraries. There are approximately 1,000 online services and 5,000 databases currently available, plus almost 500 databases available on CD-ROM. A printed bibliography can be produced. Electronic databases are especially good when researching rapidly changing high-tech subjects, such as telecommunications and biotechnology. These computer searches are more up-to-date, and in many cases, more precise. To initiate a computer search, check with the reference desk at your library. They will also be able to give you a complete rundown of the online resources available to you. Most of the major CD-ROM and online information services offer user friendly data searches that are triggered by plain English words or phrases

Electronic databases can provide great quantities of information very quickly--especially if you have a subscription to an online service or have your own CD-ROM equipment. Specific costs for personal or corporate online subscriptions depend on the type of services provided. Typically, there is a basic service fee plus "connect time" charge, ranging from free, to $15, up to $300 or more per hour. CD-ROM disks can cost anywhere from under $100 to several thousand, depending on the type and amount of information stored on them, plus frequency of updates.

There are two annual directories which are excellent sources of basic information on all online services, CD-ROM discs and databases:

Computer Readable Databases: A Directory and Data Sourcebook
By: *Kathleen Young Marcaccio, ed. (Gale Research, Inc.);* 1991.

Directory of Portable Databases
By: *Kathleen Young Marcaccio, ed. (Gale Research, Inc.);* 1991.

Electronic Online Database Services

The following vendors are several of the more popular online database services offering broad access to a variety of different databases from different sources:

BRS

By: BRS Information Technologies.

Offers over 100 online databases and is exceptionally strong in the fields of medicine, science and education. Business offerings include ABI/Inform, Harvard Business Review, and DISCLOSURE. There is also the Business Software Database, Corporate and Industry Research Reports Online, PTS PROMT, and Industry and International Standards.

BRS Information Technologies
8000 Westpark Drive
McLean, VA 22102
800/468-0908
In VA: 703/442-0900
FAX: 703/893-4632

CompuServe

By: *H&R Block.*

CompuServe is one of the world's largest online information services in terms of information available (1,400 databases) and users served (550,000 members). There are 361 pages of information sources listed in its almanac covering business, entertainment, shopping and communications needs. AP and UPI news wires are available to access the latest news, plus an electronic clipping service. CompuServe has a collection of over 850 bibliographic and full-text databases, plus comprehensive sources of demographic information. For additional information, contact:

CompuServe Information Services, Inc.
5000 Arlington Centre Boulevard
Department L, Box 477
P.O. Box 18161
Columbus, OH 43272-4630
800/848-8199
In OH: 614/457-0802

Dialog Information Services, Inc.

By: *Knight-Ridder Company.*

Dialog's extensive databank covers a wide variety of topics, with particular emphasis on business, science and technology. It covers 380 databases, 210 million records. The service provides references and abstracts of articles from more than 100,000 publications, information on more than 12 million companies and complete text of 1,000 journals and newsletters. For more information, contact:

Dialog Information Services, Inc.
3460 Hillview Avenue
Palo Alto, CA 94304
800/DIALOG (800/334-2564)
In CA: 415/858-3785
FAX: 415/858-7069

Dow Jones News/Retrieval

By: *Dow Jones, Inc.*

This is a business and financial information source which includes over 30 text and numeric databases, including 750,000 D&B reports on public and private companies, and over 20,000 analyst's research reports on companies and industries. It carries full text of back issues of The Wall Street Journal, Barron's and stories from the Dow Jones News Service. This program is menu driven and requires little instruction. For more information, contact:

Dow Jones News/Retrieval
Dow Jones & Company, Inc.
Information Services Group
P.O. Box 300
Princeton, NJ 08543-0300
800/225-3170
In NJ: 609/520-4689
FAX: 609/520-4660

Lexis/Nexis

By: *Mead Data Central (MDC).*

MDC covers 2400 databases, 85 million documents and has an active user base of over 230,000. The Lexis service is a full-text computer assisted legal research service. The Nexis service is a full-text news and business information service with more than 650 full-text sources on-line. For additional information, contact:

LEXIS/NEXIS
Mead Data Central
9393 Springboro Pike
P.O. Box 933
Dayton, OH 45401
800/227-4908
FAX: 513/865-1666

VU/TEXT

By: *Knight Ridder Company.*

The main focus of this database is on regional newspapers. It offers the full text of about 25 metropolitan papers, but it also offers stock quotes, ABI/Inform, Predicast's PROMT, and a few other bibliographic databases which are also available on other systems. For additional information, contact:

VU/TEXT Information Services, Inc.
1211 Chestnut Street
Philadelphia, PA 19107
800/258-8080
In PA: 215/665-3300

Wilsonline

By: H. W. Wilson Company.

The service offers about 20 databases--almost all of them are produced in-house and correspond to one of the printed reference works Wilson has been publishing over the years (e.g. *Business Periodical Index*). All of the databases are bibliographic in nature. Updated biweekly. For additional information, contact:

Wilsonline
H.W. Wilson Company
950 University Avenue
Bronx, NY 10452
800/367-6770
In NY: 212/588-8400

Key Business Reference Databases

The following sources are some of the more significant business databases found on CD-ROM and online information services:

ABI/Inform (CD-ROM)
By: *UMI/Data Courier.*

ABI is a bibliographic database of more than 800 business journals. Coverage is from 1971 to the present; it is updated quarterly. Records include 150 word searchable abstracts. ABI is relatively easy to use, but it requires some instruction to use effectively. For additional information, contact:

UMI Ondisc
University Microfilms International
300 North Zeeb Road
Ann Arbor, MI 48106
313/761-4700

Arthur D. Little/Online (Online Provider: DIALOG)
By: *Arthur D. Little Decision Resources.*

Provides industry forecasts, technology assessments, product and market overviews, public opinion surveys, and management commentaries. Industries and technologies covered include: Chemical, health care, pharmaceuticals, medical equipment, diagnostic products, health-care delivery services, biotechnology, advanced materials, food processing, environmental issues, information processing and telecommunications. Updated every two months.

Business Dateline (Online Providers: BRS, CompuServe, DIALOG)
By: *UMI/Data Courier.*

Full text of 110 regional U.S. and Canadian business publications as well as Crain News Service publications, nine daily newspapers and BUSINESSWIRE. Topics include regional business activity and trends, small companies, new start-ups, products and services, executives, and more. Updated weekly.

Business Periodicals Index (Online Providers: CompuServe, Wilsonline)
By: *H.W. Wilson Company.*

Index of major business magazines focusing on management, marketing, economics, industry, and finance. Corresponds to the printed version of the same title. Updated twice a week.

BUSINESSWIRE (Online Providers: CompuServe, DIALOG)
By: *BUSINESSWIRE.*
Full text of over 10,000 news sources including companies, public relations firms, government agencies, and more. Covers all types of businesses. Updated continuously.

Census I & II (CD-ROM)
By: *U.S. Bureau of the Census.*
These two disks are numeric databases produced by the U.S. Census Bureau. They include 1980 decennial population data by county and zip code and information from the 1982 censuses of manufacturing, agriculture and retailing. They are menu driven and relatively easy to use. The disks are being updated to include 1990 census data. For additional information, contact:

U.S. Bureau of the Census
Data User Services Division
Washington, D.C. 20233
301/763-2074

Corporate Affiliations (Online Providers: CompuServe,Dialog)
By: *National Register Publishing Company.*
This is a directory showing corporate family linkage and is equivalent to the printed *Corporate Affiliations*. Parent company entries show the corporate tree, while affiliate company entries show where in the corporate family they fit. Updated quarterly.

DISCLOSURE (CD-ROM)
By: *Disclosure Information Group.*
Compact disclosure is a numeric and textual database of financial and management information on over 12,000 public companies that trade stock on the NYSE, NASDAQ, the American Stock Exchange and other over-the-counter markets. It is updated bi-monthly. Disclosure includes both command and menu driven search modes. For additional information, contact:

Compact Disclosure
Disclosure Information Group
5161 River Road
Bethesda, MD 20816
800/638-8241
In MD: 301/951-1300

Dun's Million Dollar Disc (CD-ROM)
By: *Dun's Marketing Services.*
Dun & Bradstreet's electronic version of the Million Dollar Directory. Contains information on over 190,000 public and private U.S. companies having a net worth of $500,000 or more. Covers all types of commercial, industrial and business service establishments and includes headquarters, subsidiaries, and single location companies. Also contains biographical information on over 400,000 senior executives. Updated quarterly. For additional information, contact:
Dun's Marketing Services
Three Sylvan Way
Parsippany, NJ 07054-3896
800/223-1026
In NJ: 201/605-6000

Economic Literature Index (Online Providers: CompuServe, DIALOG)
By: *American Economic Association.*
An index of articles and book reviews from 260 economics journals and approximately 200 monographs per year. The *Index* corresponds to the printed quarterly index of the Journal of Economic Literature. Updated quarterly.

Encyclopedia of Associations Series (CD-ROM)
By: *Gale Research, Inc.*
This database provides access to more than 100,000 descriptive entries on over 22,000 national US associations; 60,000 regional, state, and local US associations; 97,000 international associations; and 11,000 periodicals issued by national US associations. There are 15 searchable indexes. For more information, contact:
Gale Research, Inc.
835 Penobscot Building
Detroit, MI 48226-4094
800/347-GALE (800/347-4253)
In MI: 313/961-2242
FAX: 313/961-6241

Financial World (Online Providers: CompuServe, DIALOG)
By: *DIALOG Information Services.*

Full text magazine has industry reviews, trends and forecasts, company profiles, and issues ratings. Spans 1983 to present. Updated monthly.

FINDEX (Online Providers: CompuServe, DIALOG)
By: *Information Group Directories.*
Corresponds to the printed *FINDEX: The Directory of Market Research Reports, Studies and Surveys*. Indexes and describes all such reports available for purchase from U.S. and international publishers. Also includes reports written by investment research companies on individual firms and industries. Updated twice a year.

FINIS (Online Providers: BRS, CompuServe, DIALOG)
By: *Bank Marketing Association.*
Financial Industry Information Service (FINIS), the BMA's online database contains business and financial information from over 200 publications, such as American Banker and Bank Systems + Technology. Article references, citations, abstracts and cover the last ten years. Updated every two weeks.

Forbes (Online Providers: CompuServe, DIALOG)
By: *DIALOG Information Services.*
Full text magazine covers business news, case histories, and personal profiles. Updated monthly.

Fortune (Online Providers: CompuServe, DIALOG)
By: *DIALOG Information Services.*
Full text magazine covers economic forecasts, company information, corporate performance, and personal investing. Updated monthly.

Gale GlobalAccess: Associations 1991 (CD-ROM)
By: *Gale Research, Inc.*
Contains over 80,000 descriptive entries from 3 association databases: Encyclopedia of Associations; International Organizations; Regional, State and Local Organizations of the U.S. Has a unique single-key help system for user assistance. For additional information, contact:

Gale Research, Inc.
835 Penobscot Building
Detroit, MI 48226-4094
800/347-GALE (800/347-4253)

In MI: 313/961-2242
FAX: 313/961-6241

Harvard Business Review (Online Providers: DIALOG, CompuServe, BRS)
By: *Wiley Electronic Publishingl*
Complete text of *HBR* from 1976 to date. Articles cover a broad range of business topics such as automation, business ethics, strategic planning, and more. Updated every two months.

Inc. (Online Providers: CompuServe, DIALOG)
By: *DIALOG Information Services.*
Full text magazine of small business. Topics include trends, management policies, and solutions to small business problems. Has articles on successful entrepreneurs and small businesses. Updated monthly.

Industry Data Sources (Online Providers: CompuServe and DIALOG)
By: *Information Access Company.*
Database gives primary and secondary sources of market research reports, investment banking studies, special issues of trade journals, economic forecasts, and numeric databases. Each entry includes a brief abstract and all information needed to order the report from the publisher. Updated monthly.

Industry Week (Online Providers: CompuServe, DIALOG)
By: *DIALOG Information Services.*
Business newsweekly aimed at executives; reports on all aspects of business. Updated monthly.

Information Report (Online Provider: CompuServe)
By: *NewsNet, Inc.*
Newsletter on free and low-cost business data sources such as magazines, directories, and databases provided by federal and state governments, unions and other groups. Updated monthly.

Infotrac (CD-ROM)
By: *Information Access Company.*
Used for periodical searches to find current references on

business, law, technology and the social sciences (covers 1,100 periodical listings)--one can then immediately print out a listing of relevant articles. This simple system provides easy access to desired information. Updated monthly. For more information, contact:

Information Access Company
362 Lakeside Drive
Foster City, CA 94404
800/227-8431
In CA: 415/378-5000

Innovator's Digest (Online Provider: CompuServe)
By: *NewsNet, Inc.*

Looks at the "business" of innovating. Newsletter reviews worldwide reports on innovation in many fields including technical management, marketing, and regulatory aspects of a wide range of issues. Updated every two weeks.

Investext (Online Providers: Compuserve, DIALOG)
By: *Technical Data International.*

Contains reports from more than 50 leading research firms in the U.S., Europe, Canada and Japan. Provides sales and earnings forecasts, market-share projections, research and development expenses, and similar information on over 7,500 of the largest publicly traded U.S. corporations plus 500 emerging firms. Also provides data on about 1,500 large firms listed on the European and Canadian stock exchanges. Updated weekly.

McGraw-Hill News (Online Provider: DIALOG)
By: *McGraw-Hill Information Network.*

Full text of current news stories of important business events around the world. Updated throughout the day.

Moody's Corporate News (Online Providers: CompuServe, DIALOG)
By: *Moody's Investor Services, Inc.*

The database has current, detailed coverage of business news and financial data on about 13,000 public U.S. companies. Both tabular and text records are provided on business news announcements and financial data. Updated weekly.

Nation's Business (Online Providers: CompuServe, DIALOG)
By: *DIALOG Information Services.*
Full text journal covers business news, the economy, company and management profiles, management trends, and government trends. Updated monthly.

PAIS (CD-ROM)
By: *Public Affairs Information Service.*
PAIS is a bibliographic database of domestic and international literature in the social sciences, business and government. Contains more than 300,000 citations. Coverage is from 1972 to the present with quarterly updates. For additional information, contact:
Public Affairs Information Service, Inc.
521 West 43rd Street
New York, NY 10036-4396
800/288-7247
In NY: 212/736-6629

PR Newswire (Online Provider: DIALOG)
By: *PR Newswire Association, Inc.*
Full text service of news releases from companies, public relations firms, trade associations, domestic and foreign governments, and other sources. Almost all items are business/financial in nature. Updated continually.

PTS F&S (Funk & Scott) Indexes (Online Providers: BRS, CompuServe, DIALOG)
By: *Predicasts, Inc.*
Index of data on domestic and international companies, products, and industries. Also covered are acquisitions and mergers, new products and technologies, and sociopolitical issues. Updated weekly.

PTS Marketing and Advertising Reference Service (MARS) (Online Providers: CompuServe, DIALOG)
By: *Predicasts, Inc.*
Provides data on many types of goods and services as well as the companies that provide them, their advertising agencies, advertising media, and marketing strategies. Contains abstracts from over 70 sources including key advertising journals and newsletters, consumer-oriented trade magazines, business method journals, and the advertising columns of major newspapers. Updated daily.

PTS PROMT (Online Providers: **BRS, CompuServe, DIALOG**)
By: *Predicasts, Inc.*
Predicasts Overview of Markets and Technology contains abstracts of all important information from thousands of newspapers, business magazines, trade journals, bank letters, special and government reports worldwide. Updated on a daily basis.

Standard & Poor's Economic Report (Online Provider: CompuServe)
By: *NewsNet, Inc.*
Full text service gives statistics and analysis of the economy and interest rates. Also includes predictions for major economic indicators and interest rates. Updated twice a month.

Standard & Poor's News (Online Providers: CompuServe, DIALOG)
By: *Standard & Poor's Corporation.*
Database covers general news and financial information on over 10,000 publicly owned U.S. companies on such topics as earnings, management changes, litigation, and more. Updated daily.

Standard & Poor's Register - Corporate (Online Providers: CompuServe, DIALOG).
By: *Standard & Poor's Corporation*
Contains key facts on over 45,000 U.S. public and private companies and some foreign companies with sales in excess of $1 million. Updated quarterly.

Thomas Register Online (Online Providers: CompuServe, DIALOG)
By: *Thomas Publishing Company.*
Contains full text of the printed Thomas Register of American Manufacturers, making it possible to find almost any product made in the U.S. Includes over 133,000 manufacturers of over 55,000 classes of products with over 106,000 brand names. Updated annually.

Trade & Industry Index (Online Provider: DIALOG)
By: *Information Access Company.*

Provides an index to and selected abstracts of over 300 trade and industry journals, plus selective coverage of business and trade information from an additional 1,200 publications. Also contains the *Area Business Database*, which provides indexing and abstracts from over 100 local and regional business publications. Topics include banking, insurance, agriculture, public utilities, taxation, construction, wholesale and retail trade, and more. Updated monthly.

Trademark-scan (Online provider: DIALOG)
By: Thomson & Thomson.
An excellent resource for fast single-name look-ups. Covers all trademarks currently registered with the U.S. Patent and Trademark Office. Contains 40 searchable fields, fully indexed. Separate databases for federal and state filings.

Trinet Database (CD-ROM)
By: *Trinet America, Inc.*
Contains descriptive information and total sales on more than 17 million U.S. businesses. Includes company name, address and phone number, principal officers, total sales, number of employees, SIC code, and status indicators (i.e. single location, headquarters, branch, subsidiary, public, private, or government.). Updated three times a year. For additional information, contact:

Trinet, Inc.
9 Campus Drive
Parsippany, NJ 07054
201/267-3000
FAX: 201/993-8287

Ward's Business Directory of U.S. Private and Public Companies (CD-ROM)
By: *Gale Research, Inc.*
Contains references to more than 85,000 U.S. businesses. Includes name, address, phone number, company type, executives, sales, number of employees, SIC code, and more. Corresponds to the printed 4-volume *Ward's Business Directory of U.S. Private and Public Companies.* Updated annually. For additional information, contact:

Gale Research, Inc.
835 Penobscot Building
Detroit, MI 48226-4094
800/347-GALE (800/347-4253)
In MI: 313/961-2242
FAX: 313/961-6241

Bulletin Board Services:

Online "bulletin boards" that you can access yourself with your own PC and modem are another excellent source of information. They range from the very large commercial services, such as *CompuServe, Prodigy* and *GEnie*, down to the very small services, such as a computerized database of a local business club. To list these types of resources goes far beyond the scope of this book. Numerous bulletin board directories can be found in computer periodicals, such as *Online Access*, at your local library or book store.

"Information professionals have learned over the years, how to cope with the overwhelming amount of information and reference material now available; and they have learned how to do this without squandering that most precious quantity, time."

- Sherwood Harris,
New York Public Library

DICTIONARIES AND ENCYCLOPEDIAS

The following sources provide basic definitions of terms and concepts relating to specific areas of business (such as finance, insurance, marketing or management).

Accountant's Encyclopedia
By: *Prentice Hall;* 1981.
A comprehensive desk encyclopedia addressing many conceptual and practical problems in accounting. It includes a refresher course on business mathematics.

Acronyms, Initialisms and Abbreviations Dictionary
By: *Gale Research, Inc.;* 1992.
A guide to over 500,000 terms arranged alphabetically and listed in three volumes. Covers aerospace, banking, business, government, medicine, military, science, telecommunications, transportation and other fields. There is also an international companion version.

The American Dictionary of Economics
By: *Douglas Auld (Facts on File, Inc.);* 1983.
Primarily geared toward college students majoring in economics. Treatment of entries is termed "Micro-encyclopedic."

The Arnold Encyclopedia of Real Estate
By: *Alvin L. Arnold (Warren, Gorham & Lamont);* 1980.
A very comprehensive work; entries vary from a few lines to several pages. There is an extensive appendix of charts and tables, plus a topical entry finder.

Dictionary of Banking and Finance
By: *Jerry M. Rosenberg (John Wiley & Sons);* 1985.
Utilizing short and concise definitions of over 10,000 terms, this work represents the most complete dictionary of banking and finance.

Dictionary of Business and Economics
By: *Christine and Dean Ammer (Free Press);* 1986.
The work covers a broad spectrum of terms on the theory and practice of economics and business.

Dictionary of Business and Management

By: *Jerry M. Rosenberg (John Wiley & Sons);* 1983.

Very short definitions of over 8,000 entries, covering all areas of business.

Dictionary of Business Terms

By: *Jack P. Friedman (Barron's Educational Series);* 1987.

A vest pocket-sized book of over 6,000 clear definitions of key terms used throughout the business world. Arranged alphabetically by letter (rather than word) covering the terminology of investment, banking, taxes, law, real estate, computers, management and other aspects of business.

The Dictionary of Marketing

By: *Rona Ostrow (Fairchild Publications);* 1988.

A broad, non-technical review of the terms marketers frequently encounter in direct marketing, marketing research, international marketing, advertising, sales, wholesaling and retailing. This alphabetical listing also includes principle marketing trade associations and a number of illustrative charts and graphs.

Dictionary of Marketing Terms

By: *Peter D. Bennett (Littlefield, Adams);* 1988.

Provides complete and concise definitions of over 2,000 terms and phrases used by marketing professionals. It is the most extensive reference book of marketing terms currently available.

Dictionary of Occupational Titles

By: *U.S. Department of Labor;* 1977 (w/1986 Update).

Provides comprehensive occupational descriptions and information. Used to provide the U.S. Employment Services System with standardized occupational data to assist in job placement, employment counseling and occupational and career guidance. Entries are numerically grouped by occupational type.

Dictionary of Real Estate Appraisal

By: *American Institute of Real Estate Appraisers;* 1984.

The official dictionary of the American Institute of Real Estate Appraisers. Entries are very short and frequently cross-referenced.

Economics Dictionary
By: *Donald W. Moffat (Elsevier);* 1983.
Intended as a basic text for those who study economics or related business subjects.

Encyclopedia of Associations
By: *Gale Research, Inc.;* 1991.
Three volumes. An alphabetical guide to over 22,000 national and international organizations, including trade, business, commercial and many other groups. Indexes include geographic and executive listings. The third volume lists new associations and projects.

Encyclopedia of Associations: Regional, State, and Local Organizations
By: *Gale Research, Inc.;* 1990/91.
A five-volume guide to nearly 48,000 regional, state, and local nonprofit membership organizations in all 50 states and U.S. territories. Each volume includes an alphabetical Name and Keyword Index, and is divided geographically.

Encyclopedia of Banking and Finance
By: *Glen G. Munn (Banker's Publishing Company);* 1991.
Considerably more than bare definitions of terms--illustrations with examples are used throughout. It is considered one of the best reference books in its field.

Encyclopedia of Economics
By: *Douglas Greenwald (McGraw-Hill);* 1982.
Provides in-depth coverage of over 300 subjects. Articles are lengthy, signed and provide additional references. Appendix II gives a timetable of economic events, technological developments, financial developments and economic theories.

Encyclopedia of Government Advisory Organizations
By: *Gale Research, Inc.;* 1990/91.
A listing of 6,000 entries for committees that conduct studies and organizations that advise federal officials and departments.

Encyclopedia of International Commerce
By: *William J. Miller (Cornell Maritime Press);* 1985.
Adequately covers a very complex subject area. Appendices include: statutes, symbols, directories, text material, financial and statistical data, and taxes.

Encyclopedia of Legal Information Sources
By: *Gale Research, Inc.;* 1988.
Designed for both the professional and the layperson. Under each alphabetically arranged subject heading, citations are found for a wide variety of (19) sources, both print and non-print (from statutes and laws to textbooks and audiovisuals).

Encyclopedia of Management
By: *Carl Heyel (Reinhold Publishing Corp.);* 1982.
The third revised edition is the most comprehensive; articles range from half page to 30 pages in length.

Encyclopedia of Public Affairs Information Sources
By: *Gale Research, Inc.;* 1990.
A reference guide to live, print and electronic information sources for more than 300 subjects, including organizations and agencies, journals, newsletters, annuals, bibliographies and on-line data base services.

Exporters' Encyclopedia
By: *Dun & Bradstreet;* 1990.
Provides essential importing, exporting, communications, travel and research information for about 200 world markets.

Facts on File Encyclopedia of Management Techniques
By: *Facts on File, Inc.;* 1985.
This work actually addresses techniques helpful in solving various managerial problem situations. Each entry is defined, explained, illustrated and referenced. Indexes at the end of the encyclopedia allow access to techniques by function or department and by resources to which they are applied.

The Illustrated Encyclopedic Dictionary of Real Estate
By: *Jerome S. Gross (Prentice Hall);* 1978.
This second edition includes standard terms, as well as

some of the "jargon" used in real estate. An extensive appendix of real estate forms supplements the text.

Insurance Words and Their Meanings
By: *Robert W. Strain (Rough Notes);* 1981.
This volume covers the language of property and casualty insurance. Definitions are basic and very short.

International Dictionary of Management
By: *Hano Johannsen and G. Page (Houghton Mifflin);* 1990.
Contains over 6,500 entries covering a wide range of terms which managers may come across in their daily work. Also includes a general directory of professional associations.

Kohler's Dictionary for Accountants
By: *Eric L. Kohler (Prentice Hall);* 1983.
This sixth edition is considered a standard in its field. Definitions are not limited to any standard length--more elaborate definitions are given for the more difficult concepts.

The MBI Dictionary of Modern Business Management
By: *J.A. Van Duyb (Management Books Institute);* 1990.
An alphabetical listing of business terms that provide insight and assistance on a broad range of management issues and techniques.

The MIT Dictionary of Economics
By: *David W. Pearce (MIT Press);* 1986.
Still current work; most entries are cross-referenced. Provides basic, easy to understand terminology.

The New American Dictionary of Business and Finance
By: *Jay M. Shafritz and Daniel Oran (Penguin Books);* 1990.
A pocket-sized reference book for students, business people and investors. All entries are in strict alphabetical order, and most words are cross-referenced under major headings.

Real Estate Investor's Encyclopedia
By: *Frank J. Blankenship (Prentice Hall);* 1989.
An exhaustive A-Z compilation of every term one may encounter in real estate investing.

Robert's Dictionary of Industrial Relations
By: *Harold S. Roberts (BNA, Incorporated);* 1986.
The third revised edition is the most current, and is considered the most authoritative work in its field, providing comprehensive definitions for terms used in industrial relations.

Thorndike Encyclopedia of Banking and Financial Tables
By: *David Thorndike (Warren, Gorham & Lamont);* 1987.
The encyclopedia contains financial tables for: loan payment and amortization, compound interest and annuity, interest, savings and withdrawals, installment loans, and investments. It is supplemented by an annual Yearbook (1991) featuring updated tables and reflecting current statutory changes. A detailed glossary of banking and financial terminology is also included.

Trade Names Dictionary
By: *Donna Wood (Gale Research, Inc.);* 1989.
An alphabetical guide to trade names, brand names, product names, coined names and design names, with addresses of their manufacturers, importers, marketers or distributors.

The VNR Dictionary of Business and Finance
By: *David M. Brownstone. (Van Nostrand Reinhold);* 1980.
Source book of briefly defined terms used in accounting, insurance, securities, bank consulting and advertising.

BUSINESS HANDBOOKS

Business Handbooks provide a general overview of their particular field. They are highly factual and specific sources of information that provide special value to those who need a quick refresher or overview of the industry. The following series of handbooks are some of the best published to-date. They are shown with their publication date, publisher and the author's or editor's last name).

AMA Handbook of Marketing for the Services Industry
By: *AMACOM (Congram);* 1991.

AMA Management Handbook
By: *AMACOM (Fallon);* 1983.

Banker's Handbook
By: *Dow-Jones Irwin (Baughn, Storrs and Walker);* 1988.

Business-to-Business Direct Marketing Handbook
By: *AMACOM (Ljungren);* 1989.

Compensation Handbook
By: *McGraw-Hill (Rock);* 1991.

The Complete Handbook for the Entrepreneur
By: *Prentice Hall (Brenner, Ewan and Custer);* 1990.

Eurocurrency Market Handbook
By: *New York Institute of Finance (Sarver);* 1990.

Financial Handbook for Sales and Marketing
By: *Cassell (Taylor);* 1990.

Financial Mathematics Handbook
By: *Prentice Hall (Muksian);* 1984.

Financial Planning Handbook
By: *New York Institute of Finance (Gourgues);* 1983.

Franchise Opportunities Handbook
By: *U.S. Department of Commerce;* 1988.

Franchise Opportunities Handbook: A Comprehensive Listing of the World's Leading Franchise Companies
By: *The International Franchise Association;* 1991.

Handbook for Professional Managers
By: *McGraw-Hill, Inc. (Bittel & Ramsey);* 1985.

Handbook of Accounting and Auditing
By: *Warren, Gorham and Lamont (Kay and Searfoss);* 1989.

Handbook of Budgeting
By: *John Wiley & Sons (Sweeny & Rachlin);* 1987.

Handbook of Business and Financial Ratios
By: *Prentice Hall (Tryan);* 1986.

Handbook of Business Formulas and Controls
By: *McGraw-Hill (Tucker);* 1979.

Handbook of Business Information: A Guide for Librarians, Students and Researchers
By: *Libraries Unlimited, Inc. (Strauss);* 1988.

Handbook of Business Planning and Budgeting for Executives With Profit Responsibility
By: *Van Nostrand Reinhold (Dudick);* 1983.

Handbook of Cost Accounting
By: *McGraw-Hill (Davidson and Weil);* 1978.

Handbook of Demographics for Marketing and Advertising
By: *D.C. Heath & Company (Lazer);* 1987.

Handbook of Employee Benefits
By: *Dow-Jones Irwin (Rosenberg);* 1988.

Handbook of Human Resources Administration
By: *McGraw-Hill (Famularo);* 1986.

Handbook of International Business
By: *John Wiley & Sons (Walter);* 1988.

Handbook of International Financial Management
By: *McGraw-Hill, Inc (Sweeney and Rachlin);* 1984.

Handbook of Management Consulting Services
By: *McGraw-Hill (Barcus);* 1986.

Handbook of Marketing Research
By: *McGraw-Hill (Ferber);* 1974.

Handbook of Modern Accounting
By: *McGraw-Hill (Davidson and Weil);* 1983.

Handbook of Modern Finance
By: *Warren Gorham Lamont (Logue);* 1992

Handbook of Modern Marketing
By: *McGraw-Hill (Buell);* 1986.

Handbook of Operations Research
By: *Van Nostrand Reinhold (Moder);* 1978.

Handbook of Property Management
By: *McGraw-Hill (Irwin);* 1986.

Handbook of Sales Promotion
By: *McGraw-Hill (Ulanoff);* 1985.

Handbook of Successful Franchising
By: *Liberty Hall Press (Friedlander and Gurney);* 1990.

Human Resources Management Handbook
By: *Praeger (Klarrich, Francek and Moore);* 1985.

International Finance Handbook
By: *John Wiley & Sons (George and Giddy);* 1983.

International Marketing Handbook
By: *Gale Research, Inc. (Blair);* 1988.

Little Black Book of Business Statistics
By: *AMACOM (Thomsett);* 1990.

Macmillan Small Business Handbook
By: *National Register Publishing Co. (Stevens);* 1988.

Management Development and Training Handbook
By: *McGraw-Hill (Taylor);* 1983.

Marketing Handbook
By: *Dow-Jones Irwin (Bobrow);* 1985.

The Marketing Research Handbook: A Decision Oriented Approach
By: *Prentice Hall (Ruddick);* 1985.

The Portable MBA
By: *John Wiley & Sons (Collins and Devanna);* 1990.

The Practical Guide to Joint Ventures and Corporate Alliances
By: *John Wiley & Sons (Lynch);* 1989.

Project Management Handbook
By: *Van Nostrand Reinhold (Cleland and King);* 1988.

Public Relations Handbook
By: *Dartnell (Dilenschneider);* 1987.

Sales Managers Handbook
By: *Dartnell (Riso);* 1989.

The Sales Managers Handbook
By: *Dow Jones-Irwin;* 1983.

Sales Negotiating Handbook
By: *Prentice Hall (Kellar);* 1988.

Sales Promotion Handbook
By: *Dartnell (Riso);* 1982.

Training and Development Handbook
By: *McGraw-Hill (Craig);* 1987.

EXPLANATION OF THE STANDARD INDUSTRIAL CLASSIFICATION SYSTEM

Definition
The Standard Industrial Classification System (SIC) is a numerical system designed by the U.S. Federal Government to classify and group business establishments based on their type of economic activity.

Purpose
The basic purpose of SIC coding is to facilitate the analysis, collection, tabulation and presentation of data relating to all business establishments.

Format
The SIC divides virtually all economic activity into ten major divisions:

01-09 Agriculture, Forestry and Fishing
10-14 Mining
15-17 Construction
20-39 Manufacturing
40-49 Transportation, Communication, Public Utilities
50-51 Wholesale Trade
52-59 Retail Trade
60-67 Finance, Insurance and Real Estate Services
70-89 Business Services
91-97 Health/Social Services and Public Administration

The SIC places each line of business within one of these ten divisions and assigns it a four-digit code. The first two digits broadly describe the nature of the activity (one of the ten divisions listed above). The third and fourth digits describe the activity very specifically. For example:

25 Manufacturing --Furniture and Fixtures
252 Manufacturing -- Office Furniture
2522 Manufacturing -- Metal Office Furniture

The four-digit SIC code is the most commonly used, however some systems define businesses to six or seven digits. The latest edition of the Classification Manual was up-dated and revised in 1987. The system covers 1,000 industry classifications.

Uses

The system was initially established for use by the Federal Government for statistical purposes (e.g. Bureau of the Census, in County Business Patterns). It is now widely used by individual business firms for classifying their customers and suppliers, by marketing researchers, as well as by non-government research and business organizations, and trade and professional associations which compile statistics supplementing those provided by Federal agencies (e.g. Dun & Bradstreet and Standard & Poor's, in directories of corporations). No other system is so widely used, nor does any other system describe in detail the entire U.S. economy. SIC codes truly provide the business marketer with the key to a wealth of valuable information.

Standard Industrial Classifications (SIC) Manual

By: *National Technical Information Service;* 1987.

The official U.S. government publication which identifies in detail every individual component comprising each SIC code.

BUSINESS DIRECTORIES

The following listing of business directories contains descriptive references of the most widely published and authoritatively recognized reference sources available. It should be noted that a certain amount of information overlap exists between several of the directories due to marketing competition for information services among publishers. Many of these directories are published on an annual basis.

The AMA International Membership Directory and Marketing Services Guide

By: *American Marketing Association;* 1992.

The comprehensive marketing services guide is arranged alphabetically and geographically. Specialties cover advertising, direct marketing, health care marketing, marketing consultants, marketing research, merchandising, public relations and sales promotions. Membership is listed alphabetically; an occupational listing is also provided.

America's Corporate Families and International Affiliates

By: *Dun & Bradstreet;* 1992.

Two companion volumes to the Million Dollar Directory. Volume I gives full descriptions of over 11,000 U.S. parent companies and over 55,000 subsidiaries and divisions. Volume II links 1,700 U.S. parent companies with their 13,000 foreign subsidiaries and 2,500 foreign parents with their 6,000 U.S. subsidiaries.

The Bank Quarterly

By: *Sheshunoff Information Services, Inc.;* 1990.

Provides in-depth analyses of performance and trends in the U.S. banking industry. Individual commercial and savings banks are listed alphabetically by state.

Bradford's Directory of Marketing Research Agencies and Management Consultants in the U.S. and the World

By: *Bradford's Directory of Market Research Agencies, Inc.;* 1988 (Bi-Annual).

Provides a geographic listing of marketing service agencies. Includes areas of specialty and names of top executives. The second section includes an index by type of service performed, the name of the agency and an index of personnel; an overall alphabetical index of companies is also included.

Business and Industry Directory of Greater Cincinnati
By: *Greater Cincinnati Chamber of Commerce;* 1992.
Organized alphabetically by firm name, followed by address, phone number, SIC code, description of products/services, number of employees, year established, local, national or international trade, parent company name and executive officers. NOTE: Similar directories are published by chambers of commerce for other U.S. cities.

Business Organizations, Agencies, and Publications Directory
By: *Gale Research, Inc.;* 1992.
The book includes national and international organizations, government agencies and programs, facilities and services, research, education, and publications and information services. Over 20,000 entries describe 39 types of business information sources.

Business Rankings Annual
By: *Gale Research, Inc.;* 1992.
Identifies top-ranked companies, products and services in all fields. Gives the top ten names in each of over 3,000 rankings and lists excerpted from major business publications.

Companies and Their Brands
By: *Gale Research, Inc.;* 1992.
A two volume set providing over 230,000 trade names, trademarks, and brand names of consumer oriented products and their 42,000 manufacturers, importers, marketers or distributors. All entries are in alphabetical sequence. (Also, **Brands and Their Companies.**)

Consultants and Consulting Organizations Directory
By: *Gale Research, Inc.;* 1992.
Identifies those firms and individuals active in consulting services. Each listing provides the names of top executives and a brief description of the types of services rendered and their client base. Included are indexes by subject, industries served, personnel names and names of firms.

Compu-Mark Directory of U.S. Trademarks
By: Compu-Mark U.S.; 1992.
A very thorough ten-volume index divided into two parts: one arranged by international classification, and the other alphabetically by name of trademark. Also contains a key-word index covering trademarks and registered slogans. Published annually, with quarterly updates.

The Corporate Directory
By: *Cambridge Information Group Directories, Inc.;* 1990.
Provides information on more than 10,000 publicly held U.S. corporations. Organized in two volumes and eight indexes, it supplies financial, management and stock data in broad company profiles.

Corporate Finance Bluebook
By: *National Register Publishing Co.;* 1992.
Gives an in-depth view of financial decision making personnel and outside financial service firms providing specialized financial services to more than 4,800 U.S. corporations.

Corporate Finance Sourcebook
By: *National Register Publishing Co.;* 1992.
Comprehensive directory of venture capital firms, private lenders, commercial finance and leasing companies, largest commercial banks, U.S. based foreign banks, domestic and foreign investment banks in the U.S., business intermediaries, pension managers, master trusts, cash managers, business insurance brokers, corporate real estate services and securities analysts.

The Corporate 1,000
By: *Monitor Publishing Company;* 1992.
An Alphabetical directory of those who manage the leading 1,000 companies (manufacturers, service businesses and utilities) traded on the major U.S. stock exchanges.

Corporate Technology Directory
By: *Corporate Technology Information Services, Inc.*; 1992.
A comprehensive four volume reference on over 33,000 U.S. companies that manufacture or develop high

technology products. The technologies spanned include advanced materials, automation, biotechnology, chemicals, computers, defense, energy, manufacturing, medical, pharmaceuticals, photonics, general services, software, subassemblies and components, telecommunications, tests and measurements, and transportation.

Directory of American Firms Operating in Foreign Countries
By: *World Trade Academy Press.*; 1991.
Three volume set alphabetically listing the American firms operating overseas, plus country listings giving vital statistics of these firms, including their principal product or service.

Directory of Business and Financial Services
By: *Special Libraries Association;* 1984.
Lists financial, legal and tax service businesses in the U.S. Sources are listed in a "loose-leaf" book format and are updated on a regular basis.

Directory of Corporate Affiliations (Who Owns Whom)
By: *National Register Publishing Co.;* 1992.
Gives an overview of the corporate structure of over 4,200 major US companies and their 40,000 subsidiaries, divisions and affiliates. It includes parent company vital statistics, mergers and acquisitions and name changes of companies back to 1976; also has cross reference indexes by alphabetical order, geographic location and SIC codes.

Directory of Foreign Firms Operating in the United States
By: *Uniworld Business Publications;* 1991.
Organized in two parts. Part I groups the firms by country and includes the American affiliate. Part II alphabetically lists foreign firms by name, country and the page number in Part I where the complete listing can be found.

Directory of Foreign Investment in the U.S.
By: *Gale Research, Inc.;* 1991.
Identifies over 11,000 foreign-owned real estate properties and businesses in the United States. Data is organized geographically and alphabetically, and by S.I.C. codes. Annual.

Directory of Foreign Manufacturers in the U.S.
By: *Georgia State University Press (Arpan and Ricks);* 1990.
A listing of firms operating in the U.S. owned directly or indirectly by non-U.S. companies. Recommended for its comprehensiveness and ease of use.

Directory of Management Consultants
By: *Kennedy & Kennedy, Inc. (Consultant's News)*; 1992.
A comprehensive compilation of information on over 1300 U.S. management consulting firms. Entries are listed alphabetically and cover services offered, industries served, geographic location and key executives in the firm.

Directory of Publications and Broadcast Media
By: *Gale Research, Inc.;* 1992.
A guide to over 25,000 newspapers, magazines and other periodicals, as well as over 10,000 radio, television and cable stations. Entries are arranged geographically by state and city. They contain basic descriptions, contact information, ad rates market coverage, etc.

Dun's Business Rankings
By: *Dun & Bradstreet;* 1992.
Provides comparative rankings of over 8,000 companies, both public and private, within 150 industry categories and within states.

Dun's Consultant's Directory
By: *Dun & Bradstreet;* 1992.
This work identifies and classifies 25,000 U.S. consulting firms in 200 specialties.

Dun's Directory of Service Companies
By: *Dun & Bradstreet;* 1992.
A comprehensive reference volume providing information on over 50,000 of the largest service enterprises nationwide.

Dun's Guide to Healthcare Companies
By: *Dun & Bradstreet;* 1990/91.
Provides hard-to-find data on over 15,000 healthcare manufacturers and suppliers. Includes a key-word index in professional and layman's terms, and brand name cross reference.

Dun's Regional Business Directories

By: *Dun & Bradstreet;* 1992.

Identifies approximately the top 20,000 firms in retail, wholesale, service and manufacturing markets, for each major U.S. metropolitan area.

Encyclopedia of Associations

By: *Gale Research, Inc.;* 1992.

A comprehensive listing of all types of national associations arranged by broad classifications with alphabetical and key-word indexes.

The Financial 1,000

By: *Monitor Publishing Company;* 1992.

An alphabetical listing that profiles the top US commercial banks, insurance companies, Wall Street firms and thrift institutions.

Findex: The Worldwide Directory of Market Research Reports, Studies and Surveys

By: *Cambridge Information Group;* 1992.

Covering more than 2,000 topics, this 800-page volume lists and summarizes over 13,500 "off-the-shelf" reports on worldwide market research studies on products and services. Also provides competitive industry profiles on more than 1,300 companies. Indexed by industry, subject, publisher, geography and company.

International Companies and Their Brands

By: *Gale Research, Inc.;* 1992.

A convenient resource for identifying the companies and products of the world. The book lists 15,000 international companies in a single alphabetical sort along with the 50,000 consumer products/brands they control.

The International Corporate 1,000

By: *Monitor Publishing Company;* 1992.

Organized by region, this work provides an index and profiles of those who manage the world's leading 1,000 corporations.

International Directory of Company Histories

By: *Thomas Derdak (St. James Press);* 1988.

A five volume set listing companies arranged in

alphabetical order by type of business (advertising to Utilities). Provides accurate and detailed information on the historical development of 1250 of the world's most influential companies ($2 billion in sales).

International Directory of Corporate Affiliations
By: *National Register Publishing Co.;* 1990/91.
International counterpart to the U.S. Directory of Corporate Affiliations. Gives an in-depth view of the non-U.S. holdings of U.S. parent companies, as well as U.S. and worldwide holdings of foreign enterprises. Arranged alphabetically, geographically and by SIC code.

International Directory of Marketing Research Companies and Services: The Green Book
By: *American Marketing Association, New York Chapter;* 1992.
Known in the trade as the Green Book, it provides a worldwide alphabetical listing of companies doing marketing research. In addition to company contact information, special indexes cover company services, market and industry specialty, computer programs, trademarks and service marks, geographical and telephone index and principal personnel.

The Macmillan Directory of Leading Private Companies
By: *National Register Publishing Co.;* 1992.
Provides vital statistics and financial information on over 4,300 of the largest private parent companies in the U.S. Listings are arranged alphabetically, indexes are arranged geographically and by SIC code.

Million Dollar Directory
By: *Dun & Bradstreet;* 1992.
Published in a series of five volumes, the directory provides detailed information on more than 160,000 of America's largest companies--both public and private. Includes key facts on decision-makers, company size and lines of business.

Moody's Complete Corporate Index
By: *Moody's Investors Services;* 1992.
An alphabetical index, by name, of all corporations listed in Moody's investment manuals. The manuals indexed are: Industrial, OTC, Transportation, Bank and Finance,

International and Public Utilities. The index lists only the parent companies.

National Directory of Minority-Owned and Women-Owned Business Firms

By: *Business Research Services, Inc.;* 1992.

Two separate volumes. Identifies over 40,000 firms owned by: Black Americans, Hispanic Americans, Hasidic Jews, American-Indians, Asian Pacific Americans and Women. Listings are based on SIC codes. An alphabetical index is also provided.

National Trade and Professional Associations of the United States

By: *Columbia Books;* 1992.

Alphabetical listing of over 6,000 trade, professional associations and labor unions with national membership. Indexes are provided by subject, geographic location and by acronyms used.

The Over-The-Counter 1,000

By: *Monitor Publishing Company;* 1992.

An extensive listing that covers the leading growth companies quoted on the NASDAQ exchange.

Polk's City Directories

By: *R.L. Polk & Company;* 1992.

Polk publishes more than 1400 city and suburban directories, by state. Each book is divided into four sections: 1) the buyer's guide and classified business directory, 2) an alphabetical listing of names of residents and business concerns, 3) street directory of householders and businesses and 4) a numerical telephone directory. Polk is primarily used as a prospecting tool to identify potential customers.

Pratt's Guide to Venture Capital Sources

By: *Venture Economics, Inc.* 1991.

A directory and guide to help entrepreneurs and smaller business managers understand the process of raising capital and to locate compatible venture capital investors. The text is divided into four sections: Background on Venture Capital," "How to Raise Venture Capital," "Sources of Business Development Financing" and

"Perspectives." Highlighted are small business investment companies (SBICs), which are sources of government assisted funding.

Price Waterhouse European Companies Handbook
By: *Euromoney Publications, Plc.;* 1990.
Profiles the top 2,000 companies with securities quoted on the Stock Exchanges of 18 European countries. Entries are grouped into 28 industrial sectors. Indexed by country, industry sector and alphabetically.

Principal International Businesses
By: *Dun & Bradstreet;* 1992.
International profile information on over 55,000 companies in 143 countries. Patterned after Dun's Million Dollar Directory, businesses are listed geographically, alphabetically and by SIC code.

Publishers Directory
By: *Gale Research, Inc.;* 1992.
A comprehensive source of information on over 20,000 U.S. and Canadian publishers. Covers all major publishing firms as well as small, independent presses and 550 distributors. Indexed by name, subject and geography.

Rand McNally Banker's Directory
By: *Thomson Financial Information;* 1992.
A three volume set (two U.S. and one international) profiling all chartered banks in the U.S. (and abroad), but does not include thrift institutions or Federal Reserve Banks; lists banks by state (country).

Reference Book of Corporate Managements
By: *Dun & Bradstreet;* 1992.
A four volume reference set that provides biographical profiles of principle officers and directors in more than 12,000 leading U.S. firms.

Seminars Directory
By: *Gale Research, Inc.;* 1990.
A descriptive guide to over 8,000 public seminars and workshops in 20,000 locations, covering 2,000 subject areas of interest to business, industry and government. Each entry identifies the seminar vendor, cost, location, duration

and intended audience. Includes a title index and a geographic index. Compiled by Seminar Clearinghouse International, Inc. (Second Edition).

Small Business Sourcebook
By: *Gale Research, Inc.;* 1991.
Provides resources that help small-business owners and entrepreneurs compete, such as associations, educational programs, conventions, business opportunities and government agencies. A small business profile is given for each of 194 small businesses.

Standard and Poor's Register of Corporations, Directors and Executives
By: *Standard and Poor's;* 1992.
Alphabetical list of over 45,000 U.S. and Canadian corporations. Information identifies officers, products, SIC, sales range and number of employees. Over 72,000 very short biographies of corporate executives; Who's Who in America biographical data on prominent living Americans; supplemented by Who Was Who in America, which contains sketches of prominent deceased individuals.

Standard Directory of Advertisers
By: *National Register Publishing Company;* 1992.
Known as the Advertiser Red Book, this book lists over 25,000 companies spending over $75,000 annually for national and regional advertising campaigns. Listings include name, address, type of business, key personnel, ad agencies, products advertised and medias used.

Standard Directory of Advertising Agencies
By: *National Register Publishing Company;* 1992.
Known as the Agency Red Book, entries are in alphabetical order and identify over 5,000 ad agencies, 44,000 personnel (by title), and 75,000 accounts. Entries contain number of employees, branch offices, association membership, area of specialization, annual billings, management and clients.

Standard Directory of Worldwide Marketing
By: *National Register Publishing Company;* 1992.
Known as the International Red Book, it lists advertisers

and ad agencies worldwide. All information is arranged alphabetically by company name. There are geographical indexes, as well as listings of foreign embassies and consulates in the U.S., and U.S. Embassies and consulates in other countries.

(State) Business Directory
By: *American Directory Publishing Company;* 1990/91.
The data in each of these directories comes exclusively from the Yellow Pages of each phone book published in that state. Section 1 lists businesses by Yellow Page Category; Section 2 lists manufacturers by city and product; Section 3 lists businesses by city.

(State) Industrial Directory
By: *Harris Publishing Information Services;* 1992.
Published in cooperation with state chambers of commerce, this directory is divided into five parts: county-by-county statistical information, in-depth corporate data listed alphabetically by city, index of companies by SIC codes, alphabetical listing of manufacturing companies and product/ subproduct listing of over 4,000 categories.

Thomas Register of American Manufacturers
By: *Thomas Publishing;* 1992.
The first twelve volumes list manufacturers by specific products or services. The next two volumes lists companies alphabetically and gives address, branch offices, subsidiaries, products, asset rating, and an index to product classifications; it also includes a list of leading trade names, boards of trade and chambers of commerce. The final volumes include industrial catalogs of selected companies.

U.S. Savings Institutions Directory
By: *Thomson Financial Information;* 1990.
Lists alphabetically, by state, all institutions chartered as Savings & Loans, Thrifts and Savings Banks.

Ward's Business Directory of U.S. Private and Public Companies
By: *Gale Research, Inc.;* 1992.
A comprehensive guide to over 98,000 U.S. private and public companies in alphabetical, geographical and

industrial (SIC) arrangements. Also ranks companies by sales volume within industries. Four volume set.

Who Owns Whom (North America)
By: *Dun and Bradstreet Ltd.;* 1992.
Shows the ownership of subsidiary and associate companies and how they fit into their parent groups. Parent firms are listed in alphabetical order. Each entry shows the home office address and a summary of the main business activities of the group. A separate section lists parent companies registered outside of the USA and Canada. A comprehensive alphabetical index is provided.

Who's Who in Finance and Industry
By: *Marquis--Who's Who; 1990.*
Professional profiles providing detailed information about each individual's business activities. Includes data on about 19,000 U.S. and international executives in business and business-related professions, such as stock exchanges, union leaders and selected government officials.

World Chamber of Commerce Directory
By: *Loveland Company;* 1991.
Contact information on all Chambers of Commerce, U.S. and foreign; economic development organizations; convention and visitor bureaus; state boards of tourism; U.S. and foreign embassies.

Worldwide Franchise Directory
By: *Gale Research, Inc.;* 1992.
A global directory listing approximately 2,000 American, Canadian and overseas franchises. All entries are arranged alphabetically under a primary franchise type category. Each franchise is profiled and contact information is given. Has geographic as well as keyword and name indexes.

1991-1992 Directory: Japanese Affiliated Companies in USA and Canada
By: Japan External Trade Organization. 1991.
Lists almost 10,000 Japanese affiliated companies with operations in the U.S. and Canada; covers all industries; listed and indexed alphabetically and geographically.

CORPORATE FINANCIAL INFORMATION

Two of the best sources of information on publicly held companies are corporate annual reports and 10-K reports.

Corporate annual reports are published each year by publicly held companies, primarily to provide performance information to their stockholders. Annual reports are usually supplemented by quarterly reports and investment prospectuses. Annual reports typically include the following information: corporate profile, financial highlights, message from the chief executive officer (CEO), overview of divisions/products, detailed financial review and analysis (consolidated income statements, balance sheets, cash flow statements and stockholder's equity), listing of board of directors and a verification of the financial position of the company by certified independent accountants (e.g. Price Waterhouse).

The 10-K report is the official annual business and financial report that the company must file with the U.S. Securities and Exchange Commission. It is available, usually without charge, from the company's shareholder services department.

If you are interested in obtaining current financial information on any publicly held company, simply call the corporate home office number and ask to speak to the investor relations or shareholder services department. Request that they send you a copy of their annual report, the most recent quarterly report, a prospectus and 10-K report.

Additional corporate financial information can be obtained from the following published sources.

COMPREHENSIVE INVESTMENT MANUALS & SERVICES

Moody's Bank and Finance Manual

Published in three volumes. Lists approximately 3,000 banks-with statement of accounts, history and other financial data. Also includes savings and loan associations, trust companies and federal credit agencies. Other volumes include insurance companies, unit investment trusts, investment companies, real estate companies and miscellaneous financial enterprises.

Moody's Industrial Manual

Provides facts and statistics on companies listed on the New York Stock Exchange as well as companies listed on regional American Exchanges. For each company, facts are provided on: capital structure, history, subsidiaries, joint ventures, business description, plants and properties, management, income accounts, financial and operating data, bond and stock descriptions. Statistical tables are also provided in the "Special Features" section of each volume.

Moody's International Manual

Presents financial and business information on over 5,000 corporations and national institutions in 100 countries. Corporate information includes: company history, description of business and property, financial statements, management, debt, capital and other data. National economic data is also presented.

Moody's Municipal and Government Manual

Data includes federal agencies, states, counties, cities, school districts, ports, villages and foreign governments. It presents area and population data, debt due, schedule of bonded debt, comparative statistics on finances, valuations, taxes and ratings. Also included are taxable vs. tax exempt securities and comparisons of tax exempt yields vs. government and corporations.

Moody's OTC Industrial Manual

Has the same format as Moody's Industrial Manual for those industrial corporations that are traded over-the-counter.

Moody's Public Utilities

Gives factual statistics on utility companies, including company history, management, subsidiaries, capital structure, acquisitions, contracts and franchises, long-term earnings record, rate schedules, operating data and ratios, service statistics, income and surplus accounts, and descriptions of their stocks and bonds.

Moody's Transportation Manual

Provides information on over 1,000 transportation companies including air, rail, bus lines, barge and steamship lines, oil pipelines, traction lines, tunnel, bridge and canal companies, trucking and tank car companies. It gives company history, management, details on leased lines and properties, subsidiaries, territories served, traffic statistics, financial and operating results, detailed income accounts, comparative balance sheets and Moody's rating of their bonds.

Standard & Poor's: Standard Corporation Descriptions

Very similar in scope and subject matter to Moody's Manuals. It includes a well indexed news section, with weekly and annual cumulations.

Standard & Poor's: Stock Reports

Three listing services are offered:

- The American Stock Exchange
- The New York Stock Exchange
- Over-the-Counter and Regional Exchange

This service includes approximately 4,500 companies. Each two-page company report gives statistical and descriptive data on business activities, developments, per share data, income and balance sheet data, review of operations, capital share earnings, dividend data, finances and capitalization.

The Unlisted Market Guide

This is a service, similar to Standard & Poor's Stock Reports, dealing with hard to find over-the-counter companies. Listed are both NASDOQ and non-NASDOQ companies. Indexes are provided by industry and geographic location.

Wall Street Research Reports

By: *Dow Jones & Company, Inc.*

Wall Street Corporate and Industry Research Reports are a collection of reports generated by analysts and economists from 62 major securities and institutional investment firms. (All of these reports are usually found on microfiche.)

GENERAL INVESTMENT MANUALS AND SERVICES

Corporate and Industry Research Reports
Published by J.A. Micropublishing, Inc., this is an excellent source of business/research analysts' reports on what is happening in various industries and what the outlook for the future is. The collection of reports is on microfiche and is accompanied by a printed index.

Moody's Bond Survey
Surveys the trends of the bond market and individual bonds. Includes industrial, municipal, government, corporate and commercial paper.

Moody's Dividend Record
Provides current information on dividend declarations, payment dates, ex-dividend dates, dividend meetings, income bond interest payments, payments on bonds and defaults, stock splits, stock subscription rights and preferred stocks called.

Moody's Handbook of Common Stock
Provides financial data and charts on common stocks; revised quarterly.

Standard & Poor's Bond Guide
Gives descriptions and statistical information on 15,000 corporate, municipal, convertible and industrial revenue bonds. Special features include a calendar of new offerings, a list of recent issues registered with the SEC, changes in bond quality ratings during the previous month, and S&P's Corporate and Government Bond Yield Index.

Standard & Poor's: Credit Week
Provides analysis, ratings, trends and outlook for fixed-income securities. Credit Watch provides a "watch list" which points out areas where signs of improving or declining credit quality have occurred. Credit Analysis provides detailed and concise write-ups of new issues, including the rationale behind S&P's initial rating. Credit Comment discusses the implications of economic, financial and regulatory actions on issues, industry groups and municipalities.

Standard & Poor's Outlook

A weekly publication that presents S&P's commentary on current stock market trends. It discusses individual stocks and provides recommendations. In addition, it includes articles on economic trends, change in the regulatory environment, and various developments in business and industry. The weekly statistical page includes the S&P stock price index for 96 industry groups, bond yield percentages, and the high-low-close prices for the 500 composite stock index.

Standard & Poor's: Security Owner's Stock Guide

A statistical summary of investment data on 5,300 common and preferred stocks. Included for each security are: high/low stock price range and volume, earnings per share, dividend yield, price-earnings ratio, detailed dividend information and financial position.

Value Line Investment Survey

This weekly investment advisory service comes in three sections: 1) the Summary & Index lists 1,700 stocks with their current rankings for timeliness and safety; 2) Selection & Opinion gives Value Line's opinion of the business prospect, the stock market outlook and the advisable investment strategy; 3) Ratings & Reports contains full-page reports on each of 1,700 stocks. The stocks are classified into 92 industry groups. A report on the industry precedes reports on the stocks in that industry.

"We are drowning in information,
but starved for knowledge."

- John Naisbitt,
Megatrends

INDUSTRY SOURCES

The following guides can be used to help identify information sources on specific industries.

Analyst's Handbook
By: *Standard and Poor's;* 1991.
This annual Handbook is updated by monthly supplements. Data include composite corporate per share data for over 30 years, for 72 industries. Statistics and percentages cover 13 components, including sales, operating profits, depreciation, earnings, dividends, prices, and so on.

Current Industrial Reports
By: *Department of Commerce, Bureau of the Census;* 1988.
These are specialized Census Bureau reports on various industries in the U.S. Each report presents statistics on production, shipments, exports, imports and consumption.

Directory of Industry Data Sources
By: *Ballinger Publishing Company;* 1982.
Lists references and research reports published on 4-digit SIC codes. This is the three-volume printed counterpart to the on-line data base: "Harfax."

The Encyclopedia of Business Information Sources
By: *Gale Research, Inc.;* 1991/92.
A listing of sourcebooks, periodicals, online data bases, organizations, directories, handbooks, bibliographies and other information sources, arranged by industry.

Forbes Annual Report on American Industry
By: *Forbes, Inc. (Forbes Magazine);* 1991.
Presents statistics and discussions on major industries. It provides a "yardstick of management performance," which ranks companies on the basis of profitability and growth.

Industry Review
By: *Moody's Investors Fact Sheets;* 1991.
This is a statistical service containing financial information, operating data and ratios on approximately 4,000 companies. Information is arranged by industry, in

145 industry groups, thus providing for comparisons. For each industry, a chart compares the composite stock price movements of that industry group with those of the New York Stock Exchange composite index over a 10-year period.

Industry Surveys
By: *Standard and Poor's;* 1991.
The surveys are presented in two sections, statistics and discussions on various industries. The basic analysis section gives prospects, trends, problems, statistics, tables, charts and comparative company analyses for industries and their major segments. The current analysis section gives the latest developments, as well as available industry, market and company statistics.

Predicasts Basebook
By: *Predicasts, Inc.;* 1991.
Entries reflect cyclical economic trends for products and industries. Approximately 26,000 time series are arranged by modified SIC codes. Data is collected from both government and non-government sources. The Basebook contains 15-years of annual data.

U.S. Industrial Outlook
By: *U.S. Department of Commerce;* 1990.
Covers 350 manufacturing and service industries. Gives descriptive and statistical information on current trends, recent performance, and includes industry data, product data and trade data. Each industry section contains a forecast for the coming year and a forecast over the next five years.

Value Line Investment Survey
By: *Value Line, Inc.;* 1991.
This weekly investment advisory service comes in three sections: 1) the Summary & Index lists 1,700 stocks with their current rankings for timeliness and safety. 2) Selection & Opinion gives Value Line's opinion of the business prospect, the stock market outlook and the advisable investment strategy. 3) Ratings & Reports contains full-page reports on each of 1,700 stocks. The stocks are classified into 92 industry groups. A report on the industry precedes reports on the stocks in that industry.

Wall Street Research Reports

By: *Dow Jones & Company, Inc.;* 1991.

Wall Street Corporate and Industry Research Reports are a collection of reports generated by analysts and economists from 62 major securities and institutional investment firms.

"Whether you're a politician, a general, a captain of industry - or a corporal on the way up, success almost always depends on having the right information."

- Alfred Glossbrenner, *Glossbrenner Guides*

BUSINESS RATIOS

Business performance ratios and indicators can best be found in the following sources:

Almanac of Business and Industrial Financial Ratios
By: *Prentice Hall;* 1990.
Presents two tables for each industry: Table I reports on the operating and financial information for corporations with and without net income; Table II provides the same information only for those corporations operating at a profit.

Annual Statement Studies
By: *Robert Morris Associates;* 1990.
Contains composite financial data on manufacturing, wholesaling, retailing, service and contracting lines of business. The ratios show median values as well as upper and lower quartile figures.

The Business One Irwin Business and Investment Almanac
By: *Business One Irwin (S. Levine);* 1991.
This annual almanac covers stock market averages, price/earnings ratios, futures markets, mutual fund performance, foreign stock markets, and many other topics relating to investments.

Industry Norms and Key Business Ratios
By: *Dun & Bradstreet;* 1990.
A statistical reference for evaluating and comparing financial and industrial performances of over 800 businesses nationwide. Ratios are given on solvency, efficiency and profitability. Three values are presented: upper quartile, medium and lower quartiles.

IRS Corporate Financial Ratios
By: *Schonfeld & Associates, Inc.;* 1989.
Information is based on IRS balance sheet data. The study compares ratios of companies with and without net income. The raw data used by Schonfeld is several years old.

Market Share Reporter

By: *Arson J. Darnay (Gale Research, Inc.);* 1991.

An annual compilation of reported market share data on companies, products and services. The book compiles company and product share-of-market reports from a diverse range of sources and then presents them in a graphic format. Lists over 2,000 entries arranged by SIC code. Short notes explain what is being measured and cite information sources.

Quarterly Financial Report for Manufacturing, Mining and Trade Corporations

By: *U.S. Federal Trade Commission;* 1990.

The report presents aggregate statistics on the financial results and position of US corporations. It presents estimated statements of income and retained earnings, balance sheets, and related financial and operating ratios for all manufacturing, mining and trade corporations. Data is classified by industry and by asset size.

STATISTICAL SOURCES

The following list covers both domestic and international sources of statistical, descriptive and demographic information.

DOMESTIC STATISTICAL SOURCES

American Statistics Index

By: *Congressional Information Service, Inc,;* 1990.

This is a comprehensive annual index to the statistical publications of the U.S. Government. ASI fully describes the content of those publications. The index is divided: 1) by subject, 2) by various categories such as geographic breakdown, economic breakdowns, demographic breakdowns, and 3) by various indexes such as title and Agency Report Numbers. Information is kept up-to-date with monthly supplements.

Business Statistics

By: *U.S. Department of Commerce;* 1990.

A biennial statistical supplement to the Survey of Current Business. Provides an historical record of the statistical series currently appearing in the Survey of Current Business.

Census of Manufacturers

By: *U.S. Department of Commerce;* 1987.

Information on employment, payroll, supplementary labor costs, assets, capital expenditures, rents, depreciation, inventories, cost of materials, cost and quantity of fuels consumed, value of shipments and value added by manufacturing. Figures appear in reports on industries, geographic areas, type of operation and production indexes. The Annual Survey of Manufacturers and Current Industrial Reports serve to update part of the information provided in the Census of Manufacturers.

Census of Retail Trade

By: *U.S. Department of Commerce;* 1987.

Identifies retail establishments in the U.S. Information includes number of establishments, sales, payroll and employment. Data is arranged in reports by geographic areas, by industry and by major U.S. retail centers.

Census of Service Industries

By: *U.S. Department of Commerce;* 1987.

Provides statistics on hotels, motels and other lodging places; personal and business services; automotive repair services and garages; miscellaneous repair services; amusement and recreation services, including motion pictures; health services, except hospitals; legal services; educational services, except elementary and secondary schools; colleges and universities; professional schools and junior colleges; social services; membership organizations, except labor unions, political and religious organizations. The data is presented by geographic area and by industry.

Census of Transportation

By: *U.S. Department of Commerce;* 1987.

Consists of truck inventory, usage survey and a commodity transportation survey. Figures include physical and operational characteristics of the Nation's trucks, other than those vehicles owned by Federal, State and Local governments. Also include tonnage, ton-miles, and value of commodities shipped by manufacturers. Tables also show commodity flows by SIC code of the manufacturing shipper.

Census of Wholesale Trade

By: *U.S. Department of Commerce;* 1987.

Statistics include number of establishments, sales, payroll, employment, operating expenses, and end-of-year inventories for all wholesale establishments with payroll. Has separate tabulations for merchant wholesalers, manufacturer's sales branches and offices, and merchandise agents and brokers. Data is presented by geographic area and by industry.

Additional Census Industry Reports include:

Census of Construction Industries.

Census of Mineral Industries.

Consumer USA

By: *Euromonitor Publications, Ltd.;* 1988.

Gives an overview of the U.S. Consumer Market, identifies key market segments, profiles the major U.S. consumer goods companies. Draws together all available market information on consumer trends in the U.S.

County and City Data Book

By: *U.S. Department of Commerce, Bureau of the Census;* 1988.

Provides a variety of information on states, counties, cities and places in the U.S. Data are presented on the following areas: Agriculture, area and population, banks, climate, crimes, elections, government finance and employment, health, households, housing, manufacturers, poverty retail and wholesale trade, school enrollment and other vital statistics.

County Business Patterns

By: *U.S. Department of Commerce;* 1988.

Series of publications on each state presenting data on number of business establishments, total employment and payroll by type of establishment, also economic data based on principal activity at each business location. Figures are organized based on SIC codes.

CRB Commodity Year Book

By: *Commodity Research Bureau;* 1990.

Statistical and descriptive information on 100 basic commodities. Provides ten years of annual data on: supply and distribution, production, consumption and prices.

Data Map

By: *Allison Ondrasik (Orynx Press);* 1990.

a quick guide to statistical tables covering a wide range of topics published in major statistical summaries as well as statistical periodicals of United States and international organizations.

Dun's Census of American Business

By: *Dun & Bradstreet;* 1990.

Provides summary data on the distribution of more than 8 million businesses at the national, state and county levels.

Economic Indicators

By: *U.S. Government Printing Office;* 1990.

Statistical tables and charts of basic U.S. economic indicators including total output, income and spending, employment and unemployment, production, prices, money, credit, business activity and security markets,

Federal finance and several international statistics for reference. The publication presents annual data for the last ten years, and monthly data for the most current year.

Economic Report of the President

By: *U.S. Government Printing Office;* 1991.

Includes statistical tables on national income, population, employment, wages, productivity, production, business activity, prices, money stack, credit, finance, government finance, corporate profits, agriculture, and international statistics.

Federal Reserve Bulletin

By: *U.S. Government Printing Office;* 1990.

Financial and business statistics for the U.S., plus some international statistics. Most of the data relate to finance, but indexes of industrial production, employment, construction, cost of living, retail sales and "consumer buying preferences" are of general interest. The industrial production index is one of the most widely used of all indexes.

Guide to Economic Indicators

By: *Norman Frumkin;* 1990.

A reference guide to over 50 statistical indicators of the U.S. economy (such as the GNP, interest rates, inflation, balance of payments, consumer price index, Dow-Jones, and unemployment). It provides concise and easy to understand explanations, in alphabetical order, of the basic data, their attributes, and analytical usefulness. Also includes introductory background on subjects that affect many of the indicators.

Guide to U.S. Government Statistics

By: *Documents Index, Inc.;* 1990/91.

This annual publication provides an annotated guide to 14,500 United States Government statistical publications. Arrangement of titles is by the "SuDocs" (Superintendent of Documents) classification scheme, with each entry receiving its own Documents Index cataloging number. An extensive index section references entries by agency, area, subject and title.

Handbook of Basic Economic Statistics

By: *Economic Statistics Bureau of Washington, D.C.;* 1987.

Shows current and historical statistics on industry, commerce, labor and agriculture in the U.S. Every statistical section includes comparable annual data back to 1913, or to the first year thereafter for which figures are available.

Handbook of Labor Statistics

By: *Department of Labor, Bureau of Labor Statistics;* 1989.

Produced by the Bureau of Labor Statistics, each table begins with the earliest reliable data and ends with the most current.

The Lifestyle Market Analyst

By: *Standard Rate and Data Service;* 1991.

A reference guide for consumer market analysis at the local, regional and national level. Breaks down U.S. population geographically, and demographically, and includes extensive lifestyle information on the interests, hobbies and activities popular in each market. Also helps locate consumer magazines and direct mail lists targeted to the various lifestyle profiles.

The Lifestyle Zip Code Analyst

By: *Standard Rate and Data Service;* 1991.

A very current, convenient and cost-effective reference source for anyone doing market analysis at the local level. Provides lifestyle and demographic information by zip codes.

Market Profile Analysis

By: *Dun & Bradstreet;* 1990.

Furnishes vital consumer and business demographics within every metropolitan area and/or county in the U.S.

Monthly Labor Review

By: *Department of Labor, Bureau of Labor Statistics;* 1991.

This is one of the most respected labor journals. It contains articles and statistics on employment and unemployment, hours and earnings, labor compensation, collective bargaining data, price data, productivity data, and some international comparisons.

1991 Commercial Atlas & Marketing Guide

By: *Rand McNally & Company;* 1991.

Brings together current economic and geographic information and displays them in maps, tables and charts. Divided into six sections: 1) U.S. and metropolitan area maps; 2) transportation and communication data; 3) economic data; 4) population data; 5) state maps and 6) index of statistics and places by state.

Predicasts Basebook and Forecasts

By: *Predicasts, Inc.;* 1991.

Compiles forecasts on products, markets, industry and economic aggregates for the US and North America. Shows cyclical economic trends; covers over 27,700 series. All forecasts are grouped by SIC number. An alphabetical cross reference to SIC codes appears in the appendix.

Standard & Poor's Statistical Service

By: *Standard & Poor's Corporation;* 1990.

Provides current and basic statistics on the following: banking and finance, production and labor, price indexes, income and trade, building and building materials, transportation and communication, fuels and electric power, metals, autos, rubber and tires, textiles, chemicals, paper, agricultural products and security price indexes.

State and Local Statistics Sources

By: *Gale Research, Inc.;* 1990/91.

A subject guide to statistical data on states, cities, and locales covering: agriculture, business, education, energy, environment, finance, labor, manufacturing, real estate, law enforcement, public welfare, taxation, transportation and more.

Statistical Abstract of the United States

By: *U.S. Department of Commerce;* 1990.

This is an almanac-styled statistical compendium that provides a summary of various U.S. statistical publications. Figures include population, vital statistics, immigration and naturalization, health and nutrition, education, law enforcement, courts, prisons, geography and environment, parks and recreation, elections, federal/state/local government finances and employment, national defense, social security, human services, banking, communications, energy, science and many more. Some international statistics are also shown.

Statistical Reference Index

By: *Congressional Information Service, Inc.;* 1990.

A selective guide to American statistical publications from sources other than the U.S. Government (e.g. private organizations and state governments). The SRI is broken down by subject and by various categories, such as geographic, economic and demographic breakdowns. Other indexes are provided by issuing source, and by title.

Statistics Sources

By: *Gale Research, Inc.;* 1991.

A very broad subject guide to data on industrial, business, social, educational, financial and other topics for the U.S. and selected foreign countries. Lists titles and contact information.

Survey of Buying Power Data Service

By: *Sales and Marketing Management Magazine;* 1991.

Includes data and statistics frequently used by marketing researchers. Information includes county outline maps, population and vital statistics, household income distribution, effective buying income, total retail sales and a series of four buying power index tables. It covers retail sales by twelve individual store groups and ten merchandise line categories for both the current year and the last economic census. It also gives TV market data plus metropolitan and county market projections for population, effective buying income and retail sales.

Survey of Current Business

By: *Bureau of Economic Aid;* 1990.

Monthly statistics on general business indicators, commodity prices, construction, real estate, domestic trade, the labor force, employment and earnings, finance, foreign trade, etc. Monthly statistics are cumulated in the Business Statistics publication.

U.S. Industrial Outlook

By: *U.S. Department of Commerce;* 1990.

Gives economic assumptions and projections for over 350 industries. Covers natural resources and energy, construction and related industries, industrial materials and components, information and communication, the consumer economy, transportation and travel, media and education, health care, finance and business services.

INTERNATIONAL STATISTICAL SOURCES

Area Handbook Series
By: *U.S. Secretary of the Army;* 19--(Varies)
These are national surveys on 100 countries of the world. The reports are prepared by the U.S. Department of the Army and provide a detailed analysis of social, political, and economic institutions of each country.

Comecon Data
By: *Macmillan Press, Ltd.;* 1988.
Economic information on East European block countries. Data includes: main economic indicators, production, consumption, foreign trade, finance and energy.

Consumer Europe 1991
By: *Euromonitor Publications, Ltd.;* 1991.
Draws together all available market information on consumer trends in all the major countries in Western Europe, covering all major retail items purchased for use in the European household. Also provides a range of forecasts to 1994.

Demographic Yearbook
By: *United Nation's Statistical Publications Office;* 1991.
A comprehensive collection of international demographic statistics on 220 countries. Figures are presented in two sections. The first gives world summaries basic demographic statistics, size, distribution and trends in population, birth rate, mortality rates, marriage and divorce rates. The second section identifies demographic and social characteristics, including population composition, language, religion and literacy.

The Economist Book of Vital World Statistics
By: *Times Books (Random House, Inc.);* 1990.
A richly illustrated book presenting pertinent facts and

figures on the world "Global Village." Topics covered are: demographics, economic strength, agriculture and food, industry and energy, commodities, transportation and communications, government finance, inflation and finance, trade and balance of payments, debt and aid, employment, education, health, welfare, family life and environment.

Europa Handbook

By: *Europa Publications, Ltd.;* 1989.

An international survey of countries and organizations. Each country section gives data on geography, history, government, economy, transportation, social welfare, education, tourism, defense and public holidays. A statistical section on each country provides a wide range of data on population, the economy and various industries. The directory section lists government agencies, their major officers and addresses.

European Marketing Data and Statistics

By: *Euromonitor Publications, Ltd.;* 1991.

Provides comparative statistics on 33 countries of Europe. Data includes social and economic statistics, population maps, market size, leading manufacturers, retailing, leisure, tourism and growth trends. Includes over 240 statistical tables.

Index to International Statistics (IIS)

By: *Congressional Information Service, Inc.;* 1990.

A guide to the statistical publications of international intergovernmental organizations. Indexes are divided by: Subject, name, geographic locations, issuing source, title and by publication number.

Industrial Statistics Yearbook

By: *Statistical Office of the United Nations* (2 vols.); 1987.

Contains basic data on industrial activity and structure for individual countries or areas. The second volume contains detailed information on world production of industrial commodities.

International Financial Statistics (IMF)

By: *International Monetary Fund;* 1990.

Contains world statistical tables on exchange rates,

international liquidity, money and banking statistics, interest rates, prices, production, international transactions, government finance, daily exchange rates, international reserves, changes in money and commodity prices. Individual country tables list figures on exchange rates, fund position, international liquidity, national banks, deposit money banks, monetary survey, interest rates, prices, production and employment.

International Marketing Data and Statistics

By: *Euromonitor Publications, Ltd.;* 1991.

Statistical tables on over 153 countries (arranged in 15 regional groups) listing population, standard of living, health, housing, education manpower, employment, natural resources, economy, production, consumption, and communications.

United Nations Statistical Yearbook

By: *United Nation's Statistical Publications Office;* 1987.

A basic statistical compendium of all U.N. countries. Figures cover: population, manpower, agriculture, production and consumption, mining, manufacturing, construction, energy, foreign trade, transportation, communications, balance of payments, prices and wages, national accounts, finance, development assistance, health, housing, education, culture, science and technology. This yearbook is updated by the United Nations Monthly Bulletin of Statistics.

Other U.N. Statistical Yearbooks and Reports include:
U.N. Yearbook of International Trade Statistics. 1984.
U.N. Yearbook of National Accounts Statistics. 1981.
Industry and Development Global Report. 1988/89.

The World Fact Book

By: *U.S. Central Intelligence Agency;* 1990.

Produced annually, this is a basic reference on 250 countries and other entities that also includes regional maps. Each entry gives the latest available information under the headings of geography, people, government, economy, communications and defense forces.

World Index of Economic Forecasts

By: *Gower Publishing Company (Stockholm Press);* 1988.

Includes industrial tendency surveys and development plans and lists info on over 300 organizations worldwide engaged in economic forecasting.

World Tables

By: *The World Bank;* 1990.

Provides statistics on population, national accounts, prices, balance of payments, external public debt, foreign trade indexes, central government finances, manufacturing and industrial statistics, and comparative economic data.

Worldwide Economic Indicators

By: *Business International Corp.;* 1985.

Statistical data on 131 countries. Each country profile includes: key economic indicators, GDP or NMP by activity, demographic and labor force data, wages and prices, foreign trade, miscellaneous production and consumption data.

NOTE: Additional statistical information can be found on individual countries in the form of government produced reports and annualized yearbooks as well as publications from the business sector (too numerous to mention here). Several examples of these would be:

Japan Statistical Yearbook.

Japan Economic Almanac.

Overseas Business Reports and Marketing in (France).

Statistical Abstract of Latin America.

"In the progression from information to knowledge, one must remember what Einstein said: Imagination is more important than knowledge."

- Chris Wesselman,
Research One

BUSINESS AND PROFESSIONAL PERIODICAL PUBLICATIONS BY SUBJECT

PERIODICAL LISTINGS

Trade publications such as journals, magazines and newsletters are extremely important sources of current information on issues relevant to specific industries and business areas. One of the best ways for anyone to stay current in their area of specialty is to subscribe to and read the major periodicals of their field. Also, for anyone seeking information on an industry or field with which they are unfamiliar, a quick review of the top two or three publications devoted to that specialty can be extremely helpful in providing basic information and direction.

The following list identifies a number of the more popular publications in each of fourteen business categories, ranging from accounting and banking to real estate and taxation. Although fairly broad, this list is not intended to be all-inclusive. Some states and various foreign countries have their own assortment of professional journals (too numerous to list here). For more detailed subscription information on most of the following publications, see the "Periodicals Indexed" section at the front of H.W. Wilson Company's *Business Periodical Index*.

1. ACCOUNTING

Accounting Horizons
By: *American Accounting Association;* Quarterly.
Features a variety of professional accounting articles.

Accounting Review
By: *American Accounting Association;* Quarterly.
Articles on accounting, theory, research and education.

The CPA Journal
By: *New York State Society of CPA's;* Monthly.
Journal is geared toward accounting, business finance practitioners and educators; has articles on accounting, auditing, personal financial planning, estate planning, and more.

Internal Auditor

By: *Institute of Internal Auditors, Inc.;* Monthly.

A technical journal designed to keep high-level executives abreast of current developments in theory and practice of internal auditing.

The Journal of Accountancy

By: *American Institute of CPA's;* Monthly.

Contains reports on the latest accounting views, development, management advisory services, taxation, education and professional subjects.

Management Accounting

By: *National Association of Accountants;* Monthly.

Offers the latest word on financial and accounting techniques to help companies reduce costs and increase profits.

National Public Accountant

By: *National Society of Public Accountants;* Monthly.

Exposes accountants in public practice to current thinking and practical subjects in accounting, auditing, taxes, etc.

Ohio CPA Journal

By: *Ohio Society of CPA's;* Monthly.

Has articles on current issues affecting CPA's, as well as management issues affecting business managers and CFO's. (Other states have similar journals.)

The Outlook

By: *California Society of CPA's;* Monthly.

Technical and informative articles of special interest to CPA's.

Practical Accountant

By: *Warren Gorham & Lamont;* Monthly.

Contains articles on accounting and taxes having an impact on the everyday business operations of CPA's.

Price Waterhouse Review

By: *Price Waterhouse;* Quarterly.

Contains accounting and auditing articles, profiles and statistics of interest to accountants and auditors.

2. BANKING / FINANCE / INVESTMENT

ABA Banking Journal
By: *Simmons-Boardman Publishing Corp.;* Monthly.
Has a combination of trend articles, opinion round-ups, and how-to information. Covers corporate and retail banking investments and funds management, plus new products and services for banks.

American Banker
By: *Thomson Publishing Company;* Daily.
Daily news and feature articles written to meet the working needs of bankers in the U.S.

Bank Management
By: *Bank Administration Institute;* Monthly.
Focuses on issues of interest to professionals in the field of bank management.

Bank Marketing
By: *Bank Marketing Association;* Monthly.
Covers information of interest to bankers and other financial marketing professionals.

Banker's Magazine
By: *Warren Gorham & Lamont;* Bi-monthly.
Contains insights, strategies and real-life perspectives to provide readers with an understanding of a wide range of current banking issues.

Banker's Monthly
By: *Hanover Publishers;* Monthly.
A national magazine with articles on bank management.

Banking Law Journal
By: *Warren Gorham & Lamont;* 10 issues yearly.
Practical law articles for bank legal counsel and staff.

Banking Software Review
By: *ICP, Inc,;* Quarterly.
Written for operations managers, data processing and information systems executives of commercial banks, savings and loans, and credit unions.

Barron's

By: *Dow Jones;* Weekly.

A weekly newspaper with timely articles for financial and other business executives.

Business Credit

By: *National Association of Credit Management;* 10 issues yearly.

Covers company finance, business credit and related areas with news and feature articles on credit and lending.

Corporate Cashflow

By: *Communication Channels, Inc.;* Monthly.

Publication has articles pertaining to corporate cash management issues.

Estate Planning

By: *Warren Gorham & Lamont;* Bi-Monthly.

Contains analysis of recent tax developments and legal decisions; provides guidance on estate and gift taxation, income shifting, insurance planning, and other matters.

Finance and Development

By: *International Monetary Fund;* Quarterly.

Contains articles analyzing financial and economic developments; also, explains the policies and work of the International Monetary Fund and the World Bank.

Financial Analyst's Journal

By: *Financial Analyst's Federation;* Bi-Monthly.

Contains articles on accounting, economics, ethics, securities analysis, portfolio management, securities laws and regulations.

Financial Market Trends

By: *Organization for Economic Cooperation & Development Publications;* Tri-Quarterly.

Offers comprehensive commentary on major domestic and international financial markets.

Financier

By: *Bank Administration Institute;* Monthly.

Provides a forum for financial ideas for the private sector.

Futures Magazine
By: *Oster Communications, Inc.;* Monthly.
Written for institutions and individuals interested or involved in trading futures and options on commodities and financial instruments.

Investor's Daily
By: *Investor's Daily, Inc.;* Daily.
A national business paper focusing on financial news.

Institutional Investor
By: *Capital Cities Media;* Monthly.
Financial investment magazine targeted toward top-level business and financial professionals.

Issues in Bank Regulation
By: *Bank Administration Institute;* Quarterly.
Contains articles explaining the meaning and source of current financial regulations.

Journal of Cash Management
By: *Treasury Communications;* Bi-Monthly.
Contains in-depth articles on all aspects of corporate treasury management; produces surveys and directories of banks and other vendors.

Journal of Commercial Bank Lending
By: *Robert Morris Associates;* Monthly.
Contains topics relating to various aspects of commercial lending, financial statement analysis, and credit information exchange.

Journal of Finance
By: *American Financial Association;* 5 times/yr.
A Scholarly journal covering theory and practice in the field of finance.

Journal of Money, Credit and Banking
By: *Ohio State University Press;* Quarterly.
An economics journal on monetary and fiscal policy, credit markets, money and banking.

Journal of Retail Banking
By: *Thomson Publishing Corporation;* Quarterly.

Written for professionals in the consumer financial services industry.

Mergers and Acquisitions
By: *MLR Publishing Company;* Bi-Monthly.
Contains articles on the merger/aquisitional divestiture process, plus a comprehensive record of all deals valued over $1 million.

Money
By: *Time Warner, Inc.;* Monthly.
Covers all aspects of family finance, investments, careers, shopping, taxes, insurance and consumerism.

Money Maker Magazine
By: *Consumers Digest, Inc.;* Bi-Monthly.
Written to help newly emerging investors achieve financial security.

Money World
By: *WMP Enterprises;* Monthly.
Contains a complete range of world financial and investment news for those who follow stock and commodity markets.

Mortgage Banking
By: *Mortgage Bankers Association of America;* Monthly.
Covers mortgage banking and other financial fields.

Pensions and Investment Age
By: *Crain Communications, Inc.;* Bi-Weekly.
Provides news and timely information for corporate financial executives and investment managers.

Pension World
By: *Communication Channels, Inc.;* Monthly.
Magazine for employee benefit plan sponsors and investment managers; articles focus on employee benefit plan design and administration.

Personal Investor
By: *KCI Communications, Inc.;* Bi-Weekly.
Has articles containing news and financial advice for the personal investor.

Savings Institutions

By: *U.S. League of Savings Institutions;* Monthly.

Contains news and feature articles for management personnel at all types of savings institutions.

Sylvia Porter's Personal Finance

By: *Kiplinger Washington Editors, Inc.;* 10 issues yearly.

A newsletter covering trends and strategies in personal money management.

Trusts and Estates

By: *Communication Channels, Inc.;* Monthly.

Serves the field of estate planning, and trust administration, as well as the related areas of investments, law, taxes, life insurance, accounting, property appraisal and liquidation.

United States Banker

By: *Kalo Communications, Inc.;* Monthly.

Independent national magazine targeted to CEOs and senior executives in the U.S. banking and financial community.

Value Line Investment Survey

By: *Value Line, Inc.;* Weekly.

Provides analysis and ratings of stocks across 60 industries; each issue has full-page reports on over 100 leading stocks.

Wall Street Journal

By: *Dow Jones, Inc.;* Daily.

Daily newspaper containing news, current events and other information affecting all areas of business and professional life.

Wall Street Transcript

By: *Wall Street Transcript Corp.;* Weekly.

Contains company studies, industry surveys, technical analysis and presentations by corporate officers before security analyst societies.

3. BUSINESS (General)

Across the Board

By: *Conference Board, Inc.;* Monthly.

A general interest business magazine for management and CEOs.

AT&T Toll Free 800 Directory - Business Edition

By: *AT&T Communications;* Annual.

Contains over 120,000 national toll-free telephone numbers for business-to-business calling; organized alphabetically by business name (white pages), and product or service category (yellow pages).

Balance Sheet

By: *Southwestern Publishing Company;* 5 issues yearly.

Provides business and economics educators with an open forum for discussions of business problems of current interest.

Better Investing Magazine

By: *National Association of Investors Corp.;* Monthly.

Provides investment education, ideas and techniques, news of investment clubs, plus legislative and regulatory items affecting investors.

Black Enterprise

By: *Earl G. Graves Publishing Company;* Monthly.

A business service magazine for the black entrepreneur, professional and administrator.

Boardroom Reports

By: *Boardroom Reports, Inc.;* Semi-monthly.

Provides news and information to small and mid-sized business owners and managers to help them run their businesses more effectively and efficiently.

Bottom Line/Personal

By: *Boardroom Reports, Inc.* Bi-Monthly.

Designed to help busy career people handle their personal lives more effectively. Selects and generates best possible information free from the influence of advertising.

Business Guide to Careers
By: *McGraw Hill;* Bi-Monthly.
A career and college oriented publication.

Business Opportunities Journal
By: *Business Service Corp.;* Monthly.
Contains articles specializing in real estate investing and business opportunities in the U.S. and Canada. Lists over 2,000 business franchises, distributorships and properties.

Business Today
By: *Foundation for Student Communication, Inc.;* Tri-Quarterly.
Contains articles on social responsibility of business, its relationship with government, current economic problems and policies, and more.

Business Week
By: *McGraw Hill;* Weekly.
Reports and interprets news covering all phases of business--production, labor, marketing, management, finance, research, economics, exports, transportation, labor relations and new products.

Cincinnati Business Courier
By: *American City Business Journals;* Weekly.
Contains business news, analysis and features relating to the greater Cincinnati and Northern Kentucky area (similar journals can be found in other major cities).

Communication Briefings
By: *Encoders, Inc.;* Monthly
Contains articles on all aspects of communicating, including: marketing, management, public relations, sales, and training.

Crain's (Chicago/Cleveland/Detroit/New York) Business
By: *Crain Communications, Inc.;* Weekly.
Provides in-depth coverage of metro-area business news across all industries and services.

Entrepreneur Magazine
By: *Entrepreneur Magazine;* Monthly.
Contains in-depth research and start-up details on small

businesses, like computer and book stores, fashion and image consulting.

Executive Female

By: *National Association for Female Executives;* Bi-Monthly.

Contains reports on business news, and trends as they impact women in management and women-owned businesses.

Executive Strategies

By: *National Institute of Business Management;* Monthly.

Contains articles on career growth, professional improvement and savvy tips for the business executive and professional.

Forbes

By: *Forbes Publishing Company;* Bi-Weekly.

Contains articles and news for top executives in business and finance who require information on corporate management.

Fortune

By: *Time/Warner, Inc.;* Bi-Weekly.

Aimed at top executives and upper-level managers; focuses on the ideas, issues, individuals and investments that can help them better manage their businesses and personal finances.

Franchising Opportunities Guide

By: *International Franchise Association;* Semi-Annual.

Provides a comprehensive listing and profiles of the world's leading franchise companies.

Greater Cincinnati Business Record

By: *Greater Cincinnati Business Record;* Weekly.

Provides weekly business news coverage and statistics on the greater Cincinnati and Northern Kentucky area.

Harvard Business Review

By: *Harvard Graduate School of Business Administration;* Bi-Monthly.

Contains articles written by business and business education authorities to help inform professionals of the latest developments in their fields.

Inc.

By: *Inc. Magazine;* Monthly.

Contains business articles focusing on sales and marketing issues and activities.

Industry Week

By: *Penton Publishing Company;* Bi-Weekly.

Contains articles on a variety of industry trends, news and management techniques.

National Business Woman

By: *National Federation of Business and Professional Women's Clubs;* Quarterly.

Presents articles and news of interest to working women.

Nation's Business

By: *U.S. Chamber of Commerce;* Monthly.

Provides small and mid-size business owners and managers the information they need to run a more successful business; has reports on news, trends and business issues.

PC Resource

By: *IDG Communications/Peterborough;* Monthly.

A hands-on guide to business and personal productivity. Contains non-technical articles, tips and techniques, how-to's, as well as reviews and product information to assist the PC product buyer.

Quality Digest

By: *Quality Circle Digest, Inc.;* Monthly.

Covers all areas of quality improvement: total quality management (TQM), employee involvement, SPC, and more.

Small Business Opportunities

By: *Harris Publishing, Inc.;* Bi-Monthly.

Contains articles and information for the small business entrepreneur and manager.

Success Magazine

By: *Hal Publications, Inc.;* Monthly.

A general interest management magazine with a focus on the individual effectiveness of the executive.

Women in Business

By: *American Business Women's Association;* Bi-Monthly.

Covers trends, career advancement tips, self-improvement methods, and general business news of interest to working women.

Working Woman

By: *Lang Communications;* Monthly.

Written for, by and about women business achievers; covers management, marketing, law, finance, fashion, careers, and more.

4. COMPUTERS

Adweek's Marketing Computers

By: *BPI/ASM, Inc.* Bi-Monthly.

Covers a variety of advertising and marketing issues in the high-tech industry.

Artificial Intelligence

By: *American Association for Artificial Intelligence;* Quarterly.

Designed for researchers in artificial intelligence and related fields. Contains state-of-the-art AI articles.

Automation News

By: *Grant Publications;* Bi-Weekly.

Covers automation and robotics news, as well as industry events, breakthrough, marketing and financial reports, CAD/CAM, and more.

Business Software Directory

By: *Information Sources, Inc.* Annual.

Contains entries on over 12,000 business software packages, including product name, producer name and address, description of hardware, operating system, documentation, and support.

Byte

By: *Byte Publications;* Monthly.

Written for the personal computer buyer and user; contains product and technical information.

Computer

By: *Chain Store Guide Information Services;* Weekly.

Timely news articles edited to interest micro-computer retailers and re-sellers.

Computer Decisions

By: *FM Computer Publications;* Monthly.

Contains information of interest to managers of data processing departments. Articles range from information systems to personnel management issues.

Computer Graphics World

By: *PennWell Publishing Company;* Monthly.

Covers all aspects of computer graphics hardware and software. Contains articles written by users and vendors of equipment and services of the graphics industry.

Computer Industry Report

By: *International Data Group;* Semi-Monthly.

Contains articles on market research and analysis of information processing industry; has annual census of computers as well as market projections.

Computer News International

By: *CNI Group;* Monthly.

A digest of information for high-level management executives in business, government, and education. Articles also address trade and economic issues. Bi-lingual (English/Spanish) computer magazine.

Computer Shopper

By: *Ziff Davis, Coastal Publishing;* Monthly.

An excellent source of information about direct sellers of computer products for mail order buyers.

Computerworld

By: *CW Publishing, Inc.;* Weekly.

Articles cover planning, implementation and management of corporate information systems, including data and telecommunication; includes news as well as in-depth features on everything from PCs to supercomputers.

Data Communications

By: McGraw Hill; Monthly.

Covers use, planning, design and implementation of information networks, with articles relating to efficient transmission of data including public communication services, computer networking, and more.

Datamation

By: *R.R. Bowker;* Bi-Weekly.

Contains articles and information on computers and other equipment for the information processing field; written for managers, users and consultants.

Electronic Business

By: *Cahners Publishing Company;* Bi-Weekly.

Provides ongoing information and economic analysis of the electronics industry.

Government Computer News

By: *Cahners-Ziff Computer Publishing Associates;* Bi-Weekly.

National newspaper of government computing.

Home Office Computer

By: *Scholastic, Inc.;* Monthly.

Offers a non-technical approach to a wide range of computing applications for the entire family.

IBM Systems Journal

By: *IBM Corporation;* Quarterly.

Provides techniques of practical interest to system applicators; includes technical descriptions of programming techniques, computer systems and operating systems.

Lotus

By: *Lotus Publishing;* Monthly.

Contains articles and information to help managers and professionals to use PCs and peripherals, spreadsheets and other software more creatively and productively.

Mac Guide Magazine

By: *Mac Guide Magazine, Inc.;* Monthly.

Features descriptions of various products available to users of Apple's Macintosh computer.

MacUser

By: *Ziff Davis Publishing Company;* Monthly.

Offers product reviews, techniques, and hints to increase the power and performance of the Macintosh computer.

Newmedia

By: *Hypermedia Communications, Inc.* Monthly.

Provides help to communications professionals to create products or presentations using computer animation.

Online Access

By: *Chicago Fineprint, Inc.;* Quarterly.

National magazine for business people who want to learn to use online products and services.

Online Today

By: *CompuServe, Inc.;* Monthly.

Articles show how micro-computer based communications can help increase productivity, manage resources, inform, communicate and educate.

PC Computing

By: *Ziff Davis Publishing Company;* Monthly.

Broad-based national magazine serving the needs of the computer industry.

PC Magazine

By: Ziff Davis Publishing Company; 22 issues yearly.

Independent guide to IBM standard personal computing.

PC Week

By: Ziff Davis Publishing Company; Weekly.

A weekly news journal featuring microcomputer products and developments.

PC World

By: *PCW Communications, Inc.;* Monthly.

Serves the IBM PC marketplace by helping users solve business problems and expand productivity.

Personal Computing

By: *VNU Business Publications;* Monthly.

Written for experienced business users of PCs; designed to enhance productivity through practical applications of software and computing technology.

Personal Publishing
By: *Hitchcock Publications;* Monthly.
Contains articles and information specializing in the area of desktop publishing.

Processor
By: *Peed Corporation;* Weekly.
A reliable source of information on computer products, their prices and availability.

Robotics World
By: *Communication Channels, Inc.;* Bi-Monthly.
A business magazine for industrial manufacturers in any industry that uses or has the potential for using robots or robotic systems.

Shareware Magazine
By: *PC-SIG, Inc.;* Bi-Monthly.
Periodical specifically aimed at making consumers aware of low cost/free software.

Software Magazine
By: *Sentry Publishing;* Monthly.
Offers timely articles and information on software applications and database management.

Systems Integration
By: *Cahners Publishing Company;* 16 issues yearly.
Covers DP trends and developments for micro-based computer systems.

Telecommunications
By: *Horizon House Publications, Inc.;* Monthly.
Articles cover communication technology and market development for users, service providers and manufacturers.

5. ECONOMICS / STATISTICS

American Economic Review
By: *American Economic Association;* 5 issues yearly.

Contains articles and information on economic topics of interest.

American Marketplace
By: *Business Publishers, Inc.;* Bi-Weekly.
Covers demographics, economic trends, profiles and analyses of major markets.

American Statistician
By: *American Statistical Association;* Quarterly.
A professional journal for statisticians and statistical researchers.

Atlantic Economic Journal
By: *Atlantic Economic Society;* Quarterly.
Covers all areas of theoretical and applied economics and business related topics.

Business Economics
By: *National Association of Business Economics;* Quarterly.
Contains articles on applied business economics; topics include: macro and micro economics, monetary and fiscal policy, forecasting, interest rates, international economics, and more.

Challenge
By: *M.E. Sharp, Inc.;* Bi-Monthly.
Contains a variety of articles examining economic policy issues.

Dollars and Sense
By: *Economics Affairs Bureau, Inc.;* Monthly.
Presents a wide range of economic issues from a non-technical, socialist point of view.

Economic Inquiry
By: *Western Economic Association;* Quarterly.
Presents the latest research on all topics of economics; considered one of the top economic journals.

Economic Road Maps
By: *Conference Board, Inc.;* Quarterly.
A newsletter providing graphic presentations of a wide range of general interest economic subjects.

Economics and Business

By: *Gordon and Breach Science Publishers;* Quarterly.

Designed to provide up-to-date assessments in all areas of professional economics.

Family Economic Review

By: *Agricultural Research Services;* Quarterly.

Contains articles reporting on research pertaining to the economic aspects of rural and urban family living.

Foreign Trade

By: *Defense and Diplomacy, Inc.;* Bi-Monthly.

Contains numerous short articles on international trade; a different country is profiled in each issue.

Journal of Economics and Business

By: *Springer-Verlag;* Quarterly.

A professional journal dealing with business, economics and finance.

Journal of Post-Keyensian Economics

By: *M.E. Sharp, Inc.;* Quarterly.

Provides a forum for original articles challenging existing economic theory; mainly addresses issues of the real-world and useful public policy.

Public Opinion

By: *American Enterprise Institute for Public Policy Research;* Bi-Monthly.

This publication regularly tracks American demographic and attitudinal changes on a wide variety of public policy issues.

Rand Journal of Economics

By: *Rand Corporation;* Quarterly.

This publication monitors research on the behavior of regulated industries; has articles on the economic analysis of organizations and applied micro-economics.

Small Business Economics

By: *Kluwer Academic Publishing;* Quarterly.

Provides the first forum for the economic analysis of the role of small business economics.

Survey of Current Business

By: *U.S. Superintendent of Documents;* Bi-Monthly.

Government publication containing profiles and economic analyses of businesses by types of industry.

6. HEALTH CARE

American Fitness

By: *Aerobics & Fitness Association of America;* Bi-Monthly.

A professional journal covering innovations and trends in aerobics, exercise and health.

American Health

By: *American Health Partners;* 10 issues yearly.

Designed to deal directly with current emerging lifestyles focused on individual health and well-being, nutrition, diet, beauty and active fashions.

Business

By: *Thomson Publishing Group;* Monthly.

Contains articles discussing health care cost management.

Business and Health

By: *Medical Economics Company, Inc.;* 10 issues yearly.

A magazine that covers health policy issues affecting businesses.

Ergonomics

By: *Taylor & Francis, Ltd.;* Monthly.

Information and articles evaluating human factors in relation to work environments and equipment design.

Health

By: *Family Media, Inc.;* 10 issues yearly.

Articles and information designed primarily for health-minded women.

Health Business

By: *Faulkner & Gray Healthcare Information Center;* Weekly.

Contains articles and business news covering health trends and statistics of the healthcare industry.

Health Care Management Review
By: *Aspen Publishing, Inc.;* Quarterly.
Provides authoritative and timely information on the application of sound business techniques to the administration of healthcare delivery systems.

Health Week
By: *CMP Publications;* Bi-Weekly.
Provides news analysis and feature stories for healthcare executives.

Hospitals: The Magazine for Healthcare Executives
By: *American Hospital Publishing, Inc.;* Bi-Weekly.
Provides exclusive information and news updates on today's healthcare delivery systems.

Inquiry
By: *Blue Cross and Blue Shield Association;* Quarterly.
Contains news and articles on healthcare organization, provision, and financing.

Journal of Health Care Marketing
By: *American Marketing Association;* Quarterly.
A broad-based journal for healthcare marketing professionals.

Longevity
By: *Longevity International, Ltd.;* Monthly.
A practical guide to the art and science of staying young; with articles on health, fitness, beauty, life extension and related research.

Men's Health
By: *Rodale Press;* Bi-Monthly.
Provides information for men on health, fitness, nutrition, sports, work, travel, self-care and relationships.

Modern Healthcare
By: *Crain Communications, Inc.;* Weekly.
A weekly business news magazine devoted to healthcare issues.

Nation's Health
By: *American Public Health Association;* Monthly.
Contains articles on public health policy, legislation, state policy, and more.

Occupational Hazards
By: *Penton Publishing Company;* Monthly.
Contains articles and information on health, safety and environmental management.

Safety and Health
By: *National Safety Council;* Monthly.
A magazine aimed at preventing accidents off the job and promoting health and fitness.

Strategic Health Care Marketing
By: *Health Care Communications;* Monthly.
Offers marketing strategies for hospitals, medical group practices, home health services and urgent care centers.

Today's Health
By: *Thomson Healthcare Communications;* Bi-Monthly.
A general interest periodical covering all aspects of good health.

7. INDUSTRY / TRADE

Adhesives Age
By: *Communication Channels, Inc.;* Monthly.
Contains news and technical articles for those involved in the manufacture, application, research and marketing of adhesives, sealants and related products.

Air Transport World
By: *Air Transport World;* Monthly.
A magazine on airline management throughout the world.

American Ceramic Society Bulletin
By: *The American Ceramic Society, Inc.;* Monthly.
A newsletter for professionals in the ceramics industry.

American Druggist
By: *Hearst Business Publications;* Monthly.

A magazine for pharmacists and other pharmaceutical professionals; also covers the field of wholesale drugs.

American Machinist
By: *Penton Publishing;* Monthly.
A magazine for professionals involved in technological manufacturing.

American Printer
By: *Maclean Hunter Publishing Company;* Monthly.
Covers news and articles of interest in the printing and publishing industry.

Appliance Manufacturer
By: *Cocoran Communications, Inc.;* Monthly.
A magazine with articles on appliance technology, design, manufacturing and trends.

Automation
By: *Penton Publishing;* Monthly.
A magazine of interest for engineers of factory automation technology and managers of integrated manufacturing operations.

Automotive Industries
By: *Chilton Company;* Monthly.
A magazine serving original equipment manufacturers in the automotive industry.

Automotive News
By: *Crain Communications, Inc.;* Weekly.
Tabloid reporting on all facets of the automobile and truck industry, as well as related businesses.

Aviation Week and Space Technology
By: *McGraw Hill, Inc.;* Weekly.
Contains articles and items of interest focusing on aviation and space engineering.

Beverage World
By: *Keller International Publishing Company;* Monthly.
A trade magazine for corporate executives in the multi-product beverage industry.

Broadcasting
By: *Broadcasting Publications, Inc.;* Monthly.
A news magazine covering radio, TV, cable and satellite, and the regulatory commissions involved.

Builder
By: *Hanley-Wood, Inc.;* Monthly.
Contains articles on housing, commercial and industrial building.

Builder/Dealer
By: *Peterson Brothers, Inc.;* Monthly.
A magazine serving builders, dealers and housing developers; articles focus on alternative housing construction.

Chain Store Age Executive Edition
By: *Lebhar-Friedman, Inc.;* Monthly.
A tabloid for retail store owners, operators and managers; reports on sales, marketing, merchandising and strategic planning.

Chemical and Engineering News
By: *American Chemical Society;* Weekly.
A trade journal for chemical process industries.

Chemical Business
By: *Schnell Publishing Company, Inc.;* Monthly.
Covers important long-range aspects of chemical industry management.

Chemical Engineering
By: *McGraw-Hill, Inc.;* Semi-Weekly.
A management news magazine for chemical process industries.

Chemical Week
By: *Chemical Week Assoc.;* Weekly.
Interprets the weekly news for business and technical managers in the chemical process industry.

Coal
By: *Maclean Hunter Publishing Company;* Monthly.
Contains a wide range of articles covering production,

maintenance, safety, management practices and operations of coal processing plants.

Construction Review
By: *U.S. Government Printing Office;* Semi-Monthly.
A publication listing regularly updated government statistics on the construction industry.

Control Engineering
By: *Cahners Publishing Company;* 15 times yearly.
A trade magazine for designers and users of control and instrumentation systems and related equipment.

Convenience Store News
By: *BMT Publications, Inc.;* 16 issues yearly.
A trade publication with articles and news focusing on convenience stores and gasoline marketing.

Discount Merchandiser
By: *Macfadden Holdings;* Monthly.
Contains news, feature articles, merchandising concepts and research covering the discount industry.

Discount Store News
By: *Lebhar-Friedman, Inc.;* Semi-Weekly.
Contains news and articles on new products, consumer purchasing behavior and industry reports. Targeted toward those responsible for planning, merchandising and operating retail discount stores.

Drug Topics
By: *Medical Economics Publishing Company, Inc.;* Bi-Weekly.
A retail pharmacy magazine containing news and articles on new products, merchandising techniques, and more.

Editor and Publisher Weekly Magazine
By: *Editor and Publisher Company;* Weekly.
Contains news, articles and information covering all areas of the newspaper publishing industry; also contains information on journalism, advertising and printing equipment.

Electrical World
By: *McGraw-Hill, Inc.;* Monthly.

A trade magazine covering all aspects of generating, transmitting and distributing electrical power.

Electronic Business

By: *Cahners Publishing Company;* Bi-Weekly.

Provides economic analyses of the electronic industry and offers management insight for developing business strategies.

Electronic News

By: *Fairchild Publications;* Weekly.

Articles cover the computer and electronics market; contains industry, government, military, commercial, consumer, international and aerospace news.

Electronics

By: *Penton Publishing;* Monthly.

Provides articles and reports on new electronic technical and industrial developments and trends from a global perspective.

ENR: Engineering News-Record

By: *McGraw-Hill Information Systems Company;* Weekly.

Covers all areas of engineering and construction including transportation, buildings, water supply, and related business data.

Fleet Owner

By: *FM Business Publishing, Inc.;* Monthly.

A trade magazine for owners and managers of commercial motor fleets.

Food Technology

By: *Institute of Food Technologists;* Monthly.

Provides news and technical information to assist food developers and manufacturers.

Graphic Arts Monthly

By: *Cahners Publishing Company;* Monthly.

An industry news magazine for printing and graphic arts professionals.

Grocery Marketing

By: *Gorman Publishing Company;* Bi-Weekly.

Contains a combination of news and articles on key marketing issues facing the grocery industry.

High Technology Business

By: *Infotechnology Publishing Company;* Monthly.

Contains information and news on current trends and developments across all high tech industries.

Industrial Distribution

By: *Cahners Publishing Company;* Monthly.

Covers industrial supplies; has articles on marketing, management, sales, telecommunications, computers, inventory and warehousing management.

Industry Week

By: *Penton Publishing Company;* Bi-Monthly.

A business magazine containing news and articles of interest to help executives sharpen their managerial skills and increase their effectiveness.

Interavia Aerospace Review

By: *Jane's Information Group;* Monthly.

A magazine reporting on business, commercial and military aviation developments and aerospace technology.

Lodging Hospitality

By: *Penton Publishing;* Monthly.

A management magazine with current articles and news on the hotel, motel and resort industry.

Machine Design

By: *Penton Publishing;* Bi-Monthly.

A technical magazine devoted to the design engineering function.

Manufacturing Engineering

By: *Society of Manufacturing Engineers;* Monthly.

A specialty magazine devoted to the trade of metalworking manufacturing.

Material Handling Engineering

By: *Cahners Publishing Company;* 14 issues yearly.

Written for managers of material handling systems in manufacturing plants and warehouses.

Mechanical Engineering
By: *American Society of Mechanical Engineers;* Monthly.
Contains articles on a wide range of engineering subjects, such as equipment design and production, energy transmission and plant engineering.

Meeting News
By: *Gralla Publishing;* Monthly.
Contains news, articles and new ideas to assist meeting planners set up and conduct better meetings.

Modern Office Technology
By: *Penton Publishing;* Monthly.
A trade magazine dedicated to managers of business information processing systems and equipment.

Modern Plastics
By: *McGraw-Hill, Inc.;* Monthly.
Contains news articles on developments in resin technology and other areas of the plastics industry.

Oil and Gas Journal
By: *PennWell Publishing Company;* Weekly.
A trade paper serving petroleum managers and engineers.

Packaging
By: *Cahners Publishing Company;* 14 issues yearly.
A business trade magazine for the product packaging industry.

Plant Engineering
By: *Cahners Publishing Company;* Semi-Monthly.
A technical magazine with articles and news focusing on industrial engineering.

Plastics World
By: *Cahners Publishing Company;* Monthly.
Articles present the latest information on all aspects of plastics engineering.

Professional Builder
By: *Cahners Publishing Company;* 19 issues yearly.
Covers new construction and remodeling in the housing and light construction industries; contains articles on

trends, new designs, marketing, financing, political and economic events.

Progressive Grocer
By: Maclean Hunter Media; Monthly.
Provides key information, guidance and research to grocery management; articles focus on effective food distribution and merchandising through retail outlets.

Restaurant Business
By: *Biller Communications, Inc.;* 18 times yearly.
A trade magazine for professionals in restaurants and commercial food services.

Restaurant Hospitality
By: *Penton Publishing;* Monthly.
Written for managers and other executives of commercial independent restaurants, restaurant chains, clubs, hotels and catering operations.

Supermarket Business
By: *FM Business Publishing;* Monthly.
Written for chain and independent retail and wholesale supermarket decision-makers.

Technology Review
By: *Massachusetts Institute of Technology;* 8 issues yearly.
Contains news and articles on new developments in technology, with the focus being on economic, social and political impact.

Telecommunications
By: *Horizon House-Microwave, Inc.;* Monthly.
Contains articles and news on voice, data and image communications.

Today's Office
By: *Hearst Business Publishing;* Monthly.
An executive magazine about business systems, people, equipment and technology.

Traffic Management
By: *Cahners Publishing Company;* Monthly.
News and articles cover the areas of traffic, transportation,

physical distribution and logistics.

Transportation and Distribution
By: *Penton Publishing;* Monthly.
Articles devoted to traffic and physical distribution managers and executives.

Ward's Auto World
By: *Ward's Communications, Inc.;* Monthly.
Contains news and business analysis for managers within all disciplines of the automotive industry.

World Oil
By: *Gulf Publishing Company;* Monthly.
A trade magazine on oil and gas exploration, drilling, production and distribution.

8. INSURANCE

Best's Review: Life/Health Insurance Edition
By: *A.M. Best Company;* Monthly.
Covers issues and trends within the life and health insurance industry.

Best's Review: *Property/Casualty Insurance Edition*
By: *A.M. Best Company;* Monthly.
Covers trends and issues for executives of property and casualty insurers and the agents and brokers who sell their products.

Business Insurance
By: *Crain Communications, Inc.;* Weekly.
Magazine for executives in the corporate risk, employee benefits and finance fields.

CPCU Journal
By: *The Society of CPCU;* Quarterly.
Journal containing articles and information on the property and casualty insurance business and related fields.

Insurance Advocate
By: *Chase Communications Group, Ltd.;* Weekly.

Contains legislative, regulatory, judicial and current news for the insurance industry.

Insurance Review
By: *Insurance Information Institute;* Monthly.
Contains articles for insurance agents and brokers, insurance company executives, risk managers, and others interested in the property and casualty insurance business.

Journal of CLU (Certified Life Underwriters)
By: *American Society of CLU & ChFC;* Semi-Monthly.
News and articles pertinent to the life insurance industry.

The National Underwriter
By: *National Underwriter Company;* Weekly.
One edition for news on life/health and financial services, and another edition on news and information for agents, brokers, executives and managers in property/casualty and risk/benefit insurance.

Risk Management
By: *Risk Management Society Publications, Inc.;* Monthly.
Contains articles and information focusing on insurance risk management.

Rough Notes
By: *Rough Notes Company, Inc.;* Monthly.
A sales and management magazine for property/casualty agents and brokers.

9. LABOR/HUMAN RESOURCES/EMPLOYEE RELATIONS AND BENEFITS

AFL-CIO News
By: *American Federation of Labor;* Weekly.
Provides national labor news and information on 51 state organizations.

Benefits
By: *Applied Benefits Research;* Bi-Monthly.
Features articles and information on the management of employee benefit plans.

Benefits Today
By: *Bureau of National Affairs;* Bi-Weekly.
Covers all major benefit trends including pensions, health and life insurance, dental care, medicare, and more.

Current Wage Developments
By: *U.S. Department of Labor, Bureau of Labor Statistics;* Bi-Monthly.
Reports on wage and benefit changes resulting from collective bargaining settlements and management decisions; also includes statistical summaries and reports on wage trends.

Employee Benefits Journal
By: *International Foundation of Employee Benefit Plans;* Quarterly.
Contains informative articles relating to effective management of employee benefit plans.

HR Magazine
By: *Society for Human Resource Management;* Monthly.
Provides a forum for exchange of ideas and current concepts in human resources; special topics are covered each month.

Journal of Compensation and Benefits
By: *Warren Gorham & Lamont;* Bi-Monthly.
Published for human resource professional responsible for employee benefits and compensation plans.

Journal of Labor
By: *The Journal of Labor;* Bi-Weekly.
Contains articles covering state and local news of interest to unions and union members.

Labor
By: *Labor;* Weekly.
Contains news and articles covering organized labor and the local community.

Labor Relations Week
By: *Bureau of National Affairs, Inc.;* Weekly.
Articles provide a comprehensive overview of the developments influencing private sector labor relations.

Monthly Labor Review
By: *U.S. Department of Labor;* Monthly.
Contains articles and statistics on employment and unemployment, economic growth, industrial relations, occupations, prices, productivity, safety and health, technological changes, and wages.

Negotiation Journal
By: *Plenum Publishing Company;* Quarterly.
Articles investigate the theoretical and practical developments in the field of conflict resolution.

Occupational Outlook Quarterly
By: *U.S. Superintendent of Documents;* Quarterly.
Government publication providing national occupation and employment information, issues, trends and projections.

Personnel
By: *American Management Association;* Monthly.
Covers and address every aspect of the human resource industry, including: selection, training, compensation, communications and union management.

Personnel Journal
By: *A.C. Croft, Inc.;* Monthly.
A business magazine for human resource professionals.

Steelabor
By: *United Steelworkers of America;* Monthly.
Contains news and commentary on the steel industry and members of the steelworkers union.

Training: The Magazine of Human Resource Development
By: Lakewood Publications; Monthly.
A business publication that focuses on the impact of training on human performance and productivity.

Training and Development Journal
By: *American Society for Training and Development;* Monthly.
Reports on current training and human resource practices, shares new theories and their applications, and covers controversial HR issues and subjects.

U.S. Bureau of Labor Statistics: Monthly Labor Review
By: *U.S. Bureau of Labor Statistics;* Monthly.
Government publication of charts, tables and analyses of U.S. labor and employment statistics.

Working Together
By: *Dartnell Corporation;* Semi-Monthly.
Contains articles and information focusing on improving employee/employer relations and performance, and personal career development.

10. LAW

ABA Journal: The Lawyer's Magazine
By: American Bar Association; Monthly.
Contains news articles, editorials, and features relating to law jurisprudence, the administration of justice, government, and the practice of law in general.

American Business Law Journal
By: American Business Law Association; Quarterly.
Contains manuscripts on commercial law topics including contracts, sales, anti-trust, environmental and international law book reviews and comments.

Antitrust Law and Economics Review
By: *Antitrust Law and Economics Review;* Quarterly.
Contains information on economics of industrial organization, monopoly, and competition.

Arbitration Journal
By: *American Arbitration Association;* Quarterly.
Offers articles on all forms of dispute resolution, including alternatives to litigation.

Benefits Law Journal
By: *Executive Enterprises Publications, Inc.;* Quarterly.
Contains information on new types of benefits, new methods of benefit delivery and new legal requirements.

Business Lawyer
By: *American Bar Association;* Quarterly.

Contains articles and information on topics and developments in the fields of business, banking, and corporate law.

Corporate Legal Times
By: *Giant Steps Publishing, Inc.;* Monthly.
Covers management of in-house legal departments as well as outside counsel.

Employee Relations Law Review
By: *Executive Enterprises Publications, Inc.;* Quarterly.
Contains reports and analyses of the latest laws and regulations in major areas of employee relations law; designed to meet the needs of lawyers and laymen, alike.

Estate Planning
By: *Research Institute of America;* Monthly.
A professional service that shows how to develop, implement and administer plans for virtually every estate planning situation.

Journal of Corporation Law
By: *University of Iowa, College of Law;* Quarterly.
Devoted to legal issues and problems of the modern business corporation.

Journal of Product Liability
By: *Pergamon Press;* Quarterly.
Contains articles, information, and research on all facets of product liability.

Labor Law Journal
By: *Commerce Clearing House;* Monthly.
Contains articles on the relationships of labor, union management, law and government.

Law Practice Management
By: *American Bar Association;* 8 issues yearly.
Has articles and information on law office management, systems and technology.

Legal Management
By: *Association of Legal Administrators;* Bi-Monthly.
Addresses major issues, trends, and developments on the management of delivering legal services.

National Law Journal
By: *New York Law Journal;* Weekly.
National newspaper for lawyers covering a broad range of legal issues and topics.

Official Gazette of the United States Patent and Trademark Office
By: *U.S. Patent & Trademark Office;* Weekly.
The publication is divided into two sections, one for patents and the other for trademarks. New trade names and designs are published for public opposition. Contains news on trademark laws and other current issues. Each issue is indexed. All company names cited are cumulated and published annually in the *Index to Trademarks Registered with the U.S. Patent and Trademark Office*.

Securities Regulation Law Journal
By: *Warren Gorham & Lamont, Inc.;* Quarterly.
Contains articles and regular features focusing on the changes in securities regulations, and reviews current literature in the securities field.

Tax Lawyer
By: *American Bar Association;* Quarterly.
Publication contains a variety of articles and reports on changes in U.S. tax laws.

Tort and Insurance Law Journal
By: *American Bar Association;* Quarterly.
Contains information and articles on tort and insurance law.

Trademark Register
By: *Trademark Register, Inc.;* Annual.
A cumulative listing of all currently active trademarks registered since 1881. Trademarks are not listed alphabetically, but rather by class numbers. Two companion volumes are the Trademark Owners Register and the Trademark Design Register.

Uniform Commercial Code Law Journal

By: *Warren Gorham & Lamont, Inc.;* Quarterly.

Has articles on the latest developments in laws governing commercial lending, consumer credit, and negotiable instruments.

11. MANAGEMENT

Academy of Management Review

By: *Academy of Management;* Quarterly.

Publishes theoretical, conceptual and historical issues, along with review articles, regarding management.

Advanced Management Journal

By: *Society for Advancement of Management;* Quarterly.

Offers general management articles of interest to presidents, vice presidents, and middle managers of small companies.

AMA Management Briefings

By: *American Management Association;* Monthly.

Contains articles and information concerning the day-to-day problems encountered by management.

American Journal of Small Business

By: *American Journal of Small Business;* Quarterly.

An academic journal on entrepreneurship, family-owned businesses, and small business management.

Bits and Pieces

By: *Economics Press, Inc.;* Monthly.

Designed to help managers, supervisors and executives manage their people better. Offers practical, common sense ideas to help develop and refresh management skills; filled with witty anecdotes and quotes.

Boardroom Reports

By: *Boardroom Reports, Inc.;* Semi-Monthly.

Designed to help small and mid-sized business owners and managers run their businesses more effectively and efficiently.

Bottom Line: Personal
By: *Boardroom Reports, Inc.;* Semi-Monthly.
Designed to help busy career professionals handle their personal lives more effectively; provides information from the most knowledgeable sources.

Business Week
By: *McGraw Hill;* Weekly.
A general business news magazine that reports and interprets the week's news, covers all areas of business.

CFO
By: *Economist Newspaper Group, Inc.;* Monthly.
A magazine written to serve the needs of chief financial officers; covers such general topics as: financial news and developments, insurance, cash management, taxes, benefits and accounting; also offers a buyers guide for products and services.

Chief Executive
By: *Macfadden Holdings;* Bi-Monthly.
Articles and opinions written by and for chief executives in business and industry.

Communication Briefings
By: *Encoders, Inc.;* Monthly
Contains articles on all aspects of communicating, including: marketing, management, public relations, sales, and training.

Executive Female
By: *National Association of Female Executives;* Bi-Monthly.
Magazine reports on business news and trends as they impact women in management and women-owned businesses; articles cover finance, economics, marketing strategies, demographics, corporate trends and social issues affecting businesses.

Executive Strategies
By: *National Institute of Business Management;* Monthly.
A career guide for managers and executives; articles are intended to help sharpen professional skills.

Facilities Design & Management
By: *Gralla Publications, Inc.;* Annual.
A publication for corporate executives and facility managers/planners responsible for major office complexes.

Folio: The Magazine for Magazine Management
By: *Cowles Business Media, Inc.;* Monthly.
Written for executives and other professionals in the magazine publishing industry.

Food Management
By: *Edgell Communications, Inc.;* Monthly.
A professional magazine with news and articles for the food service industry.

Hotel and Motel Management
By: *Edgell Communications, Inc.;* 8 issues yearly.
A tabloid covering news and items of interest within the lodging industry.

Human Resource Management
By: *John Wiley and Sons, Inc.;* Quarterly.
A professional journal offering information and tools for problem-solving and decision making in the human resources field.

Industrial Distribution
By: *Cahners Publishing Company;* Monthly.
A magazine covering management, marketing, sales, inventory and warehouse management of industrial supplies.

Information Executive
By: *Data Processing Management Association;* Quarterly.
A data processing journal articles and items of interest for computer and DP executives.

International Journal of Physical Distribution and Logistics
By: *MCB Publications, Ltd.;* Monthly.
A management journal concentrating on the practical applications of new ideas and strategies in the field of distribution logistics.

International Journal of Purchasing and Materials Mgmt.
By: *National Assn. of Purchasing Management;* Quarterly.
A professional trade journal for purchasing management.

Journal of Business
By: *University of Chicago Press;* Quarterly.
Contains research, analysis and articles of inquiry into theoretical and practical issues of importance to the business community.

Journal of Business Research
By: *Elsevier Science Publishing Company, Inc.;* 8 issues yearly.
Contains articles on advances in marketing and marketing research, buyer behavior, finance, risk and insurance.

Journal of Business Strategy
By: *Warren Gorham and Lamont, Inc.;* Semi-Monthly.
A general business magazine for strategic planners.

Journal of Organizational Behavior
By: *Haworth Press, Inc.;* Semi-Annual.
A professional journal devoted to issues of behavioral management in organizations.

Journal of Small Business Management
By: *Bureau of Business Research, West Virginia University;* Quarterly. Publication dedicated to the development of entrepreneurship and small business management through education, research, and the free exchange of ideas.

Journal of Systems Management
By: *Association for Systems Management;* Monthly.
Administrative planning and business systems magazine.

Journal of the American Planning Association
By: *The American Planning Association;* Quarterly.
Serves the information needs of practicing planners and educators; reviews developing theory and research, evaluates trends and methodologies.

Long Range Planning
By: *Pergamon Press;* Semi-Monthly.
A journal on strategic planning management in industry, commerce and government.

Manage
By: *National Management Association;* Quarterly.
Offers "how-to" articles on current management topics and issues of interest.

Management Review
By: *American Management Association;* Quarterly.
Covers general business and management issues of interest to executives.

Management Science
By: *The Institute of Management Science;* Monthly.
Covers all areas of interest in management science.

Management Today
By: *Management Publications Ltd.;* Monthly.
An English business publication which circulates to members of the British Institute of Management.

Management World
By: *Administration Management Society;* Semi-Monthly.
Contains articles on management trends and procedures for lower to mid-level managers.

Midwest Food Service News
By: *Target Publishing Company, Inc.;* Monthly.
A restaurant trade newspaper featuring articles on new products, services, suppliers, and other industry news.

The Office
By: *Office Publications, Inc.;* Monthly.
Articles cover office systems management and information handling; includes news on microcomputers and software, electronic mail and copying.

Operations Research
By: *Operations Research Society of America;* Semi-Monthly.
Contains information on new developments within operations research for industry professionals.

Organizational Dynamics
By: *American Management Association;* Quarterly.
A professional magazine on organizational behavior for corporate executives.

Production and Inventory Management Journal
By: *American Production and Inventory Control Society, Inc.;* Quarterly.
A professional trade journal covering production and inventory management issues and items of interest.

Public Management
By: *International City Management Association;* Monthly.
A magazine for local government administrators.

Public Personnel Management
By: *International Personnel Management Assn.;* Quarterly.
Contains articles and information for public personnel administrators responsible for selecting, hiring, training and labor relations.

Quality Review
By: *American Society for Quality Control;* Quarterly.
Presents analyses and broad application of quality improvements for managers in business, education, government, labor and communications.

Research and Development - R&D Magazine
By: *Cahners Publishing Company;* Monthly.
Written to serve research scientists, engineers, and technical managers; reports on significant advances, problems and trends that affect the performance, funding and administration of corporate R&D.

The Service Edge
By: *Lakewood Publications;* Monthly.
Newsletter focusing on creating and maintaining distinctive customer service.

Sloan Management Review
By: *Massachusetts Institute of Technology;* Quarterly.
Highlights general business trends and practical techniques for managers; also includes business case studies.

Small Business Reports
By: *American Management Association;* Monthly.
Provides articles, information and editorials for presidents, senior executives and other decision-makers of small to mid-sized firms.

Supervisory Management
By: *American Management Association;* Monthly.
A newsletter covering management and supervisory topics of interest such as performance appraisals, motivation and discipline.

Training: The Magazine for Human Resource Development
By: Lakewood Publications; Monthly.
Focuses on the impact of training on personnel performance and productivity.

Training and Development Journal
By: *American Society for Training and Development;* Monthly.
A general interest magazine on issues of human resource development and training.

12. MARKETING/MARKETING RESEARCH/ ADVERTISING & COMMUNICATIONS

Advertising Age
By: *Crain Communications;* Weekly.
Contains news and feature articles on advertising, new products, marketing and sales promotions.

Adweek's Marketing Week
By: *BPI/ASM;* Weekly.
For corporate marketing executives, has articles on new products, marketing strategies and research techniques.

American Demographics
By: *American Demographics;* Monthly.
Monitors and projects consumer trends and their effects on businesses.

Applied Marketing Research
By: *Marketing Research Association;* Quarterly.
Contains articles on statistics and marketing research.

Business Marketing
By: *Crain Communications;* Monthly.
Offers articles on techniques and methods of advertising and selling to business and industry.

Consumer Confidence Survey

By: *The Conference Board;* Monthly.

A well established 2-page newsletter reporting on consumer intentions and expectations. Surveys elicit views on general economic conditions and on short-term buying plans. Measurements include a Consumer Confidence Index and a Buying Plan Index.

Consumer Reports

By: *Consumers Union Of U.S., Inc.;* Monthly.

Product reports and ratings based on Consumers Union's tests. Has articles on health, safety, marketplace economics and legislative/regulatory actions.

DM News

By: *Mill Hollow Corp.;* Weekly.

Contains articles of interest for the direct marketing industry with news and reports on DM developments, legislation, techniques, and more.

Direct Marketing Market Place

By: *Macmillan Directory Division;* Monthly.

A reference guide to all facets of direct marketing. Has three sections: users of direct marketing techniques, suppliers, and creative consultants.

Gallup Poll Monthly

By: *The Gallup Poll;* Monthly.

Reports summary results from Gallup conducted public opinion surveys. Topics vary covering everything from religion to book buying habits. Survey sample sizes range from 1,000 to 1,500 people.

Journal of Advertising Research

By: *Advertising Research Foundation;* Monthly.

Original articles, reports and papers on advertising and marketing research, findings and conclusions.

Journal of Consumer Marketing

By: *Grayson Associates;* Quarterly.

Contains consumer-based articles targeted at the practicing marketer.

Journal of Consumer Research
By: *University of Chicago Press;* Quarterly.
Scholarly research in consumer behavior. Has empirical, theoretical and methodological articles on psychology, sociology, economics and marketing.

Journal of Marketing
By: *American Marketing Association;* Quarterly.
Contains articles on marketing discoveries, techniques, trends and new ideas.

Journal of Marketing Research
By: *American Marketing Association;* Monthly.
Provides the best available information and data on fundamental research in the areas of marketing and marketing research. Articles deal with conceptual, philosophical and technical aspects of marketing research and its various applications.

Journal of Public Policy and Marketing
By: *American Marketing Association;* Monthly.
Articles address the legal and regulatory impact of public policy on marketing activities.

Journal of Retailing
By: *New York University;* Quarterly.
Contains articles on major research, new concepts and inquiry in the field of retailing.

Marketer - The Magazine for Marketing Management
By: *Act III Publishing;* 8 issues yearly.
Conceptually explains marketing practices and how various elements affect marketing strategies.

Marketing and Media Decisions
By: *Act III Publishing;* Monthly.
Examines, evaluates and reports trends affecting national and regional marketing and media.

Marketing News
By: *American Marketing Association;* Weekly.
Contains articles on marketing and AMA activities.

Marketing Update

By: *Predicasts, Inc.;* Monthly.

Contains abstracts covering the latest news on sales, marketing and communications activities, including emerging trends and new findings in advertising, market research, public relations, new products, sales techniques, and more.

Potentials in Marketing

By: *Lakewood Publications, Inc.;* 10 issues yearly.

A marketing news magazine written for advertising, marketing, sales and sales promotion executives in business and industry.

Premium/Incentive Business

By: *Gralla Publications, Inc.;* Monthly.

Contains articles on promotional marketing stressing the use of merchandise or travel as selling and purchase incentives.

Public Relations Journal

By: *Public Relations Society of America, Inc.;* Monthly.

Covers ideas and techniques, new developments, management and communications problems for public relations executives.

Sales and Marketing Management (S&MM)

By: *Sales and Marketing Management Magazine;* Monthly.

Written for sales and marketing managers; has an annual special issue: "Survey of Buying Power" illustrating regional marketing impact of consumer purchasing patterns.

Surveys of Consumers

By: *University of Michigan Survey Research Center;* Monthly.

A 60-page newsletter reporting on general consumer confidence. Covers consumer attitudes on numerous topics. Measurements include an Index of Consumer Sentiment and an Index of Consumer Expectations (a component of the government's Index of Leading Economic Indicators).

Target Marketing

By: *North American Publishing Company;* Monthly.

Contains news, product information and articles of interest to decision makers in direct marketing, telemarketing and direct mail operations.

13. REAL ESTATE

Appraisal Journal
By: *American Institute of Real Estate Appraisers;* Quarterly.
Designed for professionals in real estate; serves as an authority on all phases of real estate valuation.

Journal of Property Management
By: *Institute of Real Estate Management;* Bi-Monthly.
Contains feature articles on real estate management, leasing and development of all property types.

Journal of Real Estate Development
By: *Federal Research Press;* Quarterly.
Comprehensive coverage of real estate development and management.

Journal of Real Estate Taxation
By: *Warren Gorham & Lamont;* Quarterly.
Contains articles on all aspects of real estate taxation.

National Real Estate Investor
By: *Commercial Channels, Inc.;* Monthly.
Considered one of the leading real estate periodicals in the U.S., it covers development, investment, financing and management of commercial real estate.

Real Estate Appraiser
By: *Society of Real Estate Appraisers;* Quarterly.
Contains articles on valuation of residential real estate and appraisal related topics.

Real Estate Tax Ideas
By: *Warren Gorham & Lamont;* 9 issues yearly.
Basically an alerting service for real estate professionals and their consultants and advisors on developments and trends in tax treatment of real estate on federal , state and local levels.

Real Estate Today

By: *National Association of Realtors;* 9 issues yearly.

Contains articles on real estate land use, brokerage trends, business systems, economics and legislative news, residential and commercial investment sales and marketing management.

14. TAXATION

Estate Planning

By: *Warren Gorham & Lamont;* Bi-Monthly.

Contains analysis of recent tax developments and legal decisions; provides guidance on estate and gift taxation, income shifting, insurance planning, and other matters.

Federal Income Tax Regulation

By: *Maxwell Macmillan Business Publications;* Monthly.

Presents the full text of income tax regulations and details regulatory activity following tax reform legislation.

Journal of Corporate Taxation

By: *Warren Gorham & Lamont;* Quarterly.

Contains articles on corporate-shareholder taxation written by distinguished authorities in the fields of tax law and accounting.

Journal of Taxation

By: *Warren Gorham & Lamont;* Monthly.

Contains in-depth analysis of new tax developments; covers all areas of taxation, including corporations, estates, trusts, partnerships, compensation, real estate and accounting.

Kiplinger Tax Letter

By: *Kiplinger Washington Editors, Inc.;* Bi-Weekly.

Service devoted exclusively to domestic tax issues--written from a non-technical viewpoint.

Review of Taxation on Individuals

By: *Warren Gorham & Lamont;* Quarterly.

A practical planning tool for professional tax advisors, suggesting long-term approaches to income, estate and gift taxation.

State Tax Review

By: *Commerce Clearing House, Inc.;* Weekly.

Highlights new state tax developments from all states, including new laws, proposed legislation, decisions, and regulations.

Tax Advisor

By: *American Institute of CPA's;* Monthly.

Contains articles on tax planning, trends and techniques.

Tax Hotline

By: *Boardroom Reports, Inc.;* Monthly.

Alerts taxpayers to opportunities and traps in the broad range of tax laws, rules and regulations that affect business operations and decisions.

Tax Management Journal

By: *Bureau of National Affairs;* Monthly.

Reviews current international tax, fiscal and economic developments affecting business operations world-wide.

Tax Planning Ideas

By: *Maxwell Macmillan Professional & Business Publications;* Semi-Monthly.

Highlights important new tax developments and analyzes their implications; explores new tax-saving angles and shows how and where to apply new tax decisions and interpretations.

Taxation for Accountants

By: *Warren Gorham & Lamont;* Monthly.

Covers current tax developments and their implications, as well as offering solutions to tax problems that frequently arise in general accounting practice.

Taxation For Lawyers

By: *Warren Gorham & Lamont;* Bi-Monthly.

Designed to help the general practice lawyer develop and maintain up-to-date tax awareness in legal matters that affect their everyday practice.

Taxes: The Tax Magazine

By: *Commerce Clearing House, Inc.;* Monthly.

Contains authoritative articles on legal, accounting, and economic aspects of federal and state taxes.

Trusts and Estates

By: Communication Channels, Inc.; Monthly.

Serves the field of estate planning, and trust administration, as well as the related areas of investments, law, taxes, life insurance, accounting, property appraisal and liquidation.

NOTE:

Many of the periodicals listed above will send you a sample copy, or even a free subscription, if you request it on your letterhead. For the addresses of these publications, and many others, consult the *1992 Standard Periodical Directory* or the *1992 Gale Directory of Publications and Broadcast Media* at your local library.

PERIODICAL SPECIAL ISSUES

A number of the major business magazines and trade publications feature special issues devoted to specific topics of interest and importance. For example, near the beginning of the year, the general-interest business publications usually run brief but informative articles profiling the "year ahead." Also, most trade journals run their own special industry-specific overviews and "largest companies" list at some point during the year.

The following is a listing of just a few of the more significant "special issues" produced by business periodicals during the course of the year. (The list is arranged alphabetically by name of periodical.)

Advertising Age

* Top 100 Leading Advertisers (July or September).
* World's Biggest Agencies (March or April).
* Nation's Top 50 Marketing Research Organizations (May).
* 100 Leading Media Companies (June)
* Top 100 Markets in the U.S.

American Banker

* 100 Largest Domestic Bank Holding Companies (March).
* 100 Largest Savings Banks in the U.S. (January).
* Top 500 Banks in the World (July).
* Top 100 Trust Banks in the U.S. (May).
* Top 300 Commercial Banks in the U.S. (March & August).
* 100 Largest Savings & Loan Associations in the U.S. (February).
* Annual Statistical Guide (December).
* Year-End Forecast Guide (December).

Banker

* Top 500 World Commercial Banks (June).

Bankers Monthly.

* Roster of Major Finance Companies (May).
* Finance and Industry Survey (May).

Best's Review

* 200 Leading Property Casualty Insurers (June).
* 500 Leading Life Insurance Companies in Total Premium Income (September).
* Leading Life Insurance Companies in: New Business Issued, Insurance In Force and Assets (July).
* Leading Companies in Credit Life Insurance (September)

Beverage World

* 100 Largest Beverage Companies (July).

Black Enterprise

* 100 Largest Black Owned Businesses (June).

Broadcasting

* Top 100 Broadcasting Companies (January).
* Top 50 Spot TV Advertisers (April).
* Top 85 Television Advertisers (May).
* Top 50 Advertising Agencies (January).
* Top 100 Companies in Electronic Communications (January).

Business Marketing

* The Leading 100 Business/Industrial Advertisers (May).
* Business/Industrial Ad Agency Roster (September).

Business Week

* Industry Outlooks (January).
* The Business Week 1,000 (April).
* Corporate Elite (Executive Compensation Survey) (April).
* Survey of R&D (July).
* Top 200 Banks (April).

Chain Store Age

* 100 Million Club (Retail Sales) (August).
* Big Builders (September).

Chemical and Engineering News

* Top 50 Chemical Firms and Products (May).
* Chemical Industry Facts and Figures (June).
* Employment Outlook (October).

Chemical Week
* Top 300 Chemical Process Industry Leaders (August).

Datamation
* Datamation 100 Largest DP Companies (June).
* Top 50 U.S. Companies in the DP Industry (May).

Discount Store News
* Annual Census of Discount Chains (July)

Editor and Publisher
* Largest 25 Circulating Newspapers (January).
* Newspaper Market Guide (October).

Electronic Business
* Annual Forecast (January)
* Electronic Business 100 (February/August).
* Electronic Business Second 100 (May/November).
* Top Electronic Companies in Europe (July).
* Top 20 Military Contractors (September).
* Top U.S. Manufacturers of Semiconductors (April).
* Top Manufacturers of Mini and Micro-Computers (September).
* Top Manufacturers of Printers (June).

Electronic Design
* Top 10 Electronic Design Firms (January).

Engineering News Record
* ENR 400 (April).
* 500 Largest Design Firms (May).
* Top International Contractors (July).

Euromoney
* Euromoney 500: Annual Ranking of the World's Largest Banks (June).

Financial World
* Economy Forecast (January).
* Financial World 500: America's Biggest Money Makers (July).
* Financial World 500: Top Growth Companies Above $25 Million in Sales (July or August).
* Annual Report Award (November).

Forbes

* Forbes Annual Report on American Industry (January).
* 25 Largest Savings and Loans (April).
* 100 Largest Bank Holding Companies (April).
* 50 Largest Trust Companies (April).
* Forbes 500 - Company Rankings by Sales, Assets, Profits and Market Value (May).
* Forbes 500 Largest Employers (May).
* 125 Largest International Businesses (July).

Fortune

* Economic Forecast (January).
* Fortune 500 List of Largest U.S. Industrial Corporations (May).
* Fortune 500 List of Largest U.S. Corporations (June).
* Fortune 500 List of Largest Foreign Corporations (August).
* Fortune Service 500: Largest U.S. Non-Industrial Corporations (June).
* 50 Largest Commercial Banks (July).
* 50 Largest Commercial Banks Outside the U.S. (August).
* Top 50 Exporters (August).
* 50 Largest Diversified Financial Companies (July).
* 50 Largest Life Insurance Companies (July).
* 50 Largest Utilities Companies (July).
* 50 Largest Retailing Companies (July).
* 50 Largest Transportation Companies (July).
* Products of the Year (December).

The Greater Cincinnati Business Record

* The Record Registry Book of Business Lists (July)

Inc.

* Inc. 100 Fastest-Growing Small Public Companies (May).
* Executive Compensation Survey (September)
* Report on the States (October).
* Inc. 500: America's Fastest Growing Private Companies (Dec.).

Industry Week

* Economists Business Outlook (September).

Institutional Investor

* America's Biggest Brokers/Investment Bankers (April).
* Global Banking Rankings (July).
* Institutional Investor's 300: Ranking America's Top Money Managers (August).

National Underwriter

* Domestic Market Report (January).
* Top 20 Auto Insurers (May).

Nations Business

* Economic Forecast (January).

Marketing News

* Marketing Research (May).
* Marketing Software (June).

Paper Trade Journal

* Top 50 Papermakers (June).

Pension and Investment Age

* Top 1,000 Funds/Sponsors (January).
* Managers Ranked By Tax-Exempt Assets (April).
* Directory of Investment Advisors (April).
* Investment Brokerage Research Survey (September).

Savings and Loan News

* Top 200 Largest Savings and Loan Associations (February/March).

Restaurants and Institutions

* Annual Report (January).
* Top 400 (July).

Sales and Marketing Management (S&MM)

* Survey of Selling Costs (February).
* Annual Survey of Consumer Buying Power (August).

Stores

* Top 100 Department Stores (July).
* Top 100 Specialty Chains (August).

Supermarket News

* Market Profiles (July or August).

NOTE:

If you are unfamiliar with the leading journals of a particular industry, refer to *Standard Rate and Data Service - Business Publications*. It is an excellent resource in assessing the depth and breadth of various publications, as well as other media. Although intended to be used as a reference for publication advertising rates, SRDS has an easy-to-use format and provides short circulation profiles of each periodical listed, including its basic purpose and intended target audience of readers. For additional information, contact:

Standard Rate & Data Service, Inc.
3004 Glenview Road
Wilmette, IL 60091-9970
800/323-4588
708/256-8333
FAX: 708/441-2252

Also, to find out when other special issues appear, consult the Special Libraries Association's *Guide to Special Issues and Indexes of Periodicals*. It will list, under the name of a periodical, the title and month of publication of a special issue.

"Your ability to manage information will be crucial to your success, whether you are an employee of a major corporation, an entrepreneur, a student or an unemployed person (either by choice or circumstance)."

- John H. Everett,
Information Broker

BUSINESS CAREERS, JOBS AND OCCUPATIONS

Researching The Job Market:

The following list of books are excellent sources of information on career development for graduates looking to move into the business world, and for job-seeking professionals already in the business sector looking to make a position or career change.

Career Employment Opportunities Directory
By: *Alvin Renetzky (Ready Reference Press);* 1985.
Volume II: Business Administration gives opportunities for employment by various U.S. companies and includes subject and geographic indexes.

Careers and the MBA
By: *B. Adams, Inc.;* 1990.
Provides articles on how to choose the right job, and profiles different companies offering jobs in business. Also includes reports on various industries and their outlook for the 1990's.

College Placement Annual: Administration, Business, and Other Non-Technical Options
By: *College Placement Council;* 1989/90.
Current information describing general employment opportunities with major corporations. Material is indexed by geographic area, occupation, and by the type of degree one holds.

The Directory of Executive Recruiters
By: *Kennedy & Kennedy, Inc.;* 1992.
Known as the "Red Book" of executive recruiters, this guide is designed to function as a workbook as well as a continuing reference. It lists profiles of over 2,000 firms and offices offering "executive search" services. It is divided into three major parts: 1) background information, 2) listing of retainer recruiting firms (those that are paid by companies on an on-going basis for their services) and 3) a listing a contingency recruiting firms (those that get paid only after a specific job placement). Listings are alphabetical.

The Directory of Outplacement Firms

By: *Kennedy & Kennedy, Inc.;* 1990/91.

Firms are listed in two sections: Section I profiles those firms retained by corporate clients only, Section II profiles firms retained by individuals, as well (firms working only for individuals are not included). Articles on outplacement services are also presented.

Dun's Career Guide

By: *Dun & Bradstreet;* 1990.

Describes career opportunities and hiring practices of more than 5,000 companies currently seeking job applicants and resumes.

Encyclopedia of Careers and Vocational Guidance

By: *J.G. Ferguson Publishing Company;* 1990.

Information is presented in a four volume set:

Volume 1 provides industry profiles and reviews various career fields;

Volume 2 describes professional, administrative and managerial occupations;

Volume 3 covers general clerical occupations;

Volume 4 deals with technical or specialized careers.

Hoover's Handbook 1992

By: *Gary Hoover (The Reference Press, Inc.);* 1992.

Profiles over 500 major corporations around the world, arranged alphabetically. Each one-page entry contains basic information on the nature of the enterprise, its history, the people who run it, the products/services delivered, and its financial performance. Information is also arranged into four additional indexes: 1) by industry, 2) by geography, 3) by corporate executives and 4) an alphabetical summary index. It is an excellent resource for job hunting and interviewing--especially for the person not familiar with business terms or protocol.

Job Hunter's Resources Guide

By: *Gale Research, Inc.;* 1990.

The central part of this guide is "Sources of Job Hunting Information: 150 Professions and Occupations," which lists job hunting manuals, directories, employment agencies, placement services, trade journals with help-wanted ads and other information services.

Jobs '92

By: *Kathryn & Ross Petras (Prentice Hall Press);* 1992.

Excellent career opportunity source book for the '90's. Gives career outlooks, industry forecasts and regional round-ups to keep one appraised of the most current trends and where they are creating jobs.

The National Job Bank

By: *B. Adams, Inc.;* 1992.

This book is a guide to major employers in the U.S. The arrangement is by state, with indexes by type of occupation within each state. Every entry gives the types of jobs available and the name of the company contact person.

Occupational Outlook Handbook

By: *U.S. Department of Labor, Bureau of Labor Statistics;* 1990/91.

This is an excellent source book for vocational guidance. It describes the nature of what workers do in each job listed, the training and education they need, earnings, working conditions, and expected job prospects for selected occupations covering a wide cross-section of the economy.

The 100 Best Companies to Sell For

By: *Michael D. Harkavy (Wiley and Sons);* 1989.

Covers the most prominent companies in eighteen leading industries. Provides 2-3 page narrative descriptions and vital statistics on 100 top firms.

The 100 Best Companies to Work For in America

By: *Robert Levering (New American Library);* 1987.

An alphabetical listing and description of 100 companies that go beyond giving their employees good pay and strong benefits --they emphasize the "human condition" by treating their people well.

Peterson's Job Opportunities for Business and Liberal Arts Graduates

By: *Peterson's Guides;* 1991.

Helps recent college graduates with their job hunting by providing an overview of the various types of employment opportunities available with 400 corporations planning to hire business and social sciences/humanities graduates.

Professional Careers Sourcebook

By: *Gale Research, Inc.;* 1992.

Presents more than 110 professional career profiles, along with related basic reference guides, handbooks and trade periodicals. Excellent for deciding on career paths to take after graduation. Master alphabetical index lists publications, organizations and other information sources.

WEEKLY PERIODICALS:

American Employment Weekly

By: *Scott Publishing;* 1992.

A selected compilation of professional career development opportunities from each of the week's Sunday edition of major newspapers across America. Positions are organized by 18 job-type categories.

The National Ad Search

By: National Ad Search, Inc.; 1992.

A compilation of employment ads placed in over 75 different newspapers across the United States. Positions are organized into over 50 job categories.

The Wall Street Journal National Business Employment Weekly

By: *Dow Jones & Company, Inc.;* 1992.

A compilation of employment ads placed in each regional edition of the Wall Street Journal. Includes articles on interviewing, resumes and job hunting techniques.

Note:

The advantage of these three publications is that you do not have to buy 80 metropolitan newspapers to scan the job postings. However, there is at least a one week time lag between when an advertised position first appears in a local or regional paper and when it is picked up by either of the above publications. The down side is that many positions are often filled by the time you see the ad. It behooves you to check out the Sunday classified sections of your local metropolitan paper, the *Sunday New York Times* for eastern U.S. coverage, the *Sunday Los Angeles Times* for western U.S. coverage, and the Tuesday *Wall Street Journal* for regional, national and international coverage. Also, certain weekly national trade publications, such as *Advertising Age* and the *Marketing News*, can be excellent job hunting sources.

MISCELLANEOUS INFORMATION SOURCES

Valuable information can be derived from many other sources than the ones already listed in preceding pages. A few of these additional sources are as follows.

BIBLIOGRAPHIES

American Marketing Association: Bibliography Series.
By: *The American Marketing Association.*
The AMA provides annotated bibliographies on a variety of marketing topics. Several examples are:

- An Annotated and Extended Bibliography of Health Care Marketing.
- An Annotated and Extended Bibliography of Higher Education Marketing.
- An Annotated Bibliography for Marketing to an Older Population.
- A Basic Bibliography on Experimental Design in Marketing.
- Marketing 2000: Future Perspectives on Marketing, An Annotated Bibliography.
- Services Marketing: An Annotated Bibliography.
- Pricing Policies and Strategies, An Annotated Bibliography.

AMACOM Management Briefings and Reports.
By: *The American Management Association.*
Several examples of these briefings and reports are:

- Strategic Pricing.
- Creating Profitable New Products and Markets.
- The Marketing Path to Global Profits.
- Value Analysis.
- Teleconferencing.
- The Leveraged Buyout.
- Total Financial Planning.

International Business Bibliography.
By: *Michael Z. Brooke (Praeger).*

Organizations, Management and Control: An Annotated Bibliography.
By: *Russell Stout, Jr.*

Small Business Bibliography.
By: *U.S. Small Business Administration.*

BIOGRAPHICAL SOURCES

The following reference sources list names, professions, and short biographies of key business leaders and corporate executives.

Reference Book of Corporate Management
By: *Dun & Bradstreet;* 1990.
Short biographical profiles of principle officers and directors in more than 12,000 leading U.S. companies, contained in four volumes.

Marquis Who's Who Publications/Index to Books
By: *Marquis Who's Who, Inc.;* 1990.

Who's Who in Advertising
By: *Marquis Who's Who, Inc.;* 1990/91.

Who's Who in American Banking
By: *American Banker (Gale Research, Inc.);* 1991.

Who's Who in Black Corporate America
By: *Who's Who in Black Corporate America;* 1982.

Who's Who in Consulting
By: *Gale Research, Inc.;* 1990.

Who's Who in Direct Marketing Creative Services
By: *WMW! Books;* 1990.

Who's Who in Economics
By: *MIT Press;* 1986.

Who's Who in Federal Government Prime Contractors
By: *Business Research Services;* 1990.

Who's Who in Finance and Industry
By: *Marquis Who's Who, Inc.;* 1992/93.

Who's Who in HR
By: *Society for Human Resources Management;* 1990.

Who's Who in Insurance
By: *Underwriter Printing and Publishing Company;* 1990.

Who's Who in Technology
By: *Gale Research, Inc.;* 1989.

Who's Who in the Lodging Industry
By: *American Hotel and Motel Association;* 1989.

Who's Who in U.S. Executives
By: *Who's Who in U.S. Executives, Inc.;* 1989.

Who's Who in Venture Capital
By: *David A. Silver (Wiley);* 1987.

Who's Wealthy in America
By: *The Taft Group;* 1990.

FEDERAL GOVERNMENT: SELECTED DEPARTMENTS AND AGENCIES

Washington DC is truly the information capital of the world. The Federal Government spends a tremendous amount of money annually accumulating information and expertise. Over 700,000 government workers gather information on almost every topic imaginable. In fact, the largest publisher in the entire world is the United States Government Printing Office (GPO). Also, federal agencies have in-house experts on almost every topic imaginable, and most are quite willing to share their knowledge and expertise.

The following directory is one of the best all-around guides to the federal government power structure:

The Washington Information Directory

By: *Congressional Quarterly, Inc.;* 1992.

Briefly describes government and non-government organizations arranged by subject. Includes listings of executive agencies, trade associations, labor unions, consumer groups foreign embassies, and more. Published annually.

The Federal Information Center is a telephone service set up to assist the public in locating government information. When called, **FIC** operators will direct you to a specific agency office for additional information on your subject. You can find the phone number of the Center closest to you by looking under the federal government listings in your local telephone book, or call the general information operator at 800/872-3362.

The following publications are just a few of the many printed guides to federal information services:

United States Government Manual

By: U.S. Office of the Federal Register; 1992.

Profiles the various agencies and departments of the judicial, executive and legislative branches. Contains organizational charts, names, titles, addresses and phone numbers of key personnel. Also has a subject/agency name index, a personnel index and assorted appendices. Published annually.

How to Find Business Intelligence in Washington

By: *Washington Researchers;* 1991.

A general directory of federal agencies that collect business-related information. Entries include contact information on each major agency and sub-agency. Supplemental sections list regional offices, libraries, documents rooms and significant publications.

Federal Statistical Directory

By: *William R. Evinger (Oryx Press);* 1991.

Lists all of the key executive agencies that gather and distribute statistical information. Arranged by agency, entries identify and provide contact data on over 4,000 agency personnel. The major focus is on the information series or publication specific areas are responsible for. Updated irregularly.

The following is a list of key departments and government agencies.

Departments/Bureaus

Department of Agriculture:
- Food and Consumer Services

Department of Commerce:
- Bureau of the Census
- Bureau of Economic Analysis
- National Bureau of Standards

Department of Defense:
- International Security Affairs

Department of Education:
- Office of Educational Research

Department of Energy:
- Technical Services Division
- Office of Energy Research

Department of Health & Human Services:
- Food & Drug Administration

Department of Housing & Urban Development

Department of the Interior:
- National Park Service

Department of Justice:
- Federal Bureau of Investigation (FBI)
- Deputy/Associate Attorney General

Department of Labor:
- Bureau of Labor Statistics
- Occupational Safety & Health Administration (OSHA)

Department of State:
- Country Desk Officers
- Public Information Service

Department of Transportation:
- Federal Aviation Administration (FAA)
- Federal Highway Administration
- Federal Railroad Administration
- National Highway Traffic Safety
- U.S. Coast Guard

Department of the Treasury:
- Bureau of Engraving and Printing
- U.S. Mint
- Internal Revenue Service (IRS)
- U.S. Secret Service

Administrative Agencies

Consumer Product Safety Commission
Environmental Protection Agency
Federal Communications Commission
Federal Emergency Management Agency
Federal Trade Commission
General Services Administration
National Aeronautics & Space Administration
National Foundation on the Arts & Humanities
National Science Foundation

National Transportation Safety Board
Small Business Administration
U.S. International Trade Commission

One of the best government information resource guides published to-date is the following:

Information U.S.A.
By: *Matthew Lesko (Viking Press);* 1986.
An extraordinarily comprehensive guide on how to get information from the US Government. It provides names, addresses and phone numbers of over 10,000 government offices and 3,000 data experts. It also lists titles of over 3,000 publications and provides access to government statistics and market research.

Another excellent source of information is the **National Reference Center** at the Library of Congress in Washington, DC. The **NRC** acts as a no-charge clearing center for information requests by referring the requestor to one of over 13,000 organizations and individuals, both public and private, who can supply data and information on specialized topics. The **NRC** can be contacted at: 202/287-5670.

LEGISLATIVE AND ADMINISTRATIVE REGULATORY SOURCES

The following sources are helpful in locating current federal legislation, texts of statutes and legislative history of statutes. They will also help in locating bills, acts, resolutions, committee prints, senate and house reports, senate and house documents, and administrative regulation.

Congressional Index
By: *Commerce Clearing House.*

CIS/Index
By: *Congressional Information Service.*

U.S. Code Congressional and Administrative News
By: *West Publishing Company.*

U.S. Statutes at Large
By: *U.S. Government Printing Office.*

The Congressional Record and its Index
By: *U.S. Government Printing Office.*

CQ: Congressional Quarterly Weekly Report
By: *Congressional Quarterly, Inc.*

The National Journal
By: *National Journal, Inc. (Times Mirror Company).*

Code of Federal Regulation
By: *Congressional Information Service.*

Law and Legal Information Directory
By: *Gale Research, Inc. (Wasserman/O'Brien)*

State Legislative Sourcebook 1991: A Resource Guide to Legislative Information in the Fifty States.
By: *Lynn Hellebust.*

Washington Information Directory
By: *Congressional Quarterly, Inc.*

STATE/LOCAL GOVERNMENT

Oftentimes information from state and local governments may not be as readily available as federal data, however these sources of information should not be discounted. The state commerce department, department of state, attorney general's office and state regulated banking and insurance commissions can be excellent sources of local business information. All states publish a variety of directories and manuals (often called "blue books"), and many other publications and documents.

The following publications are excellent beginning resources for state-related information:

State Data and Database Finder
By: *Information U.S.A., Inc.;* 1989.
Describes the various kinds of data collected by state governments. Arranged by subject, covering 38 different topics. Describes numerous databases maintained by state agencies and their availability to the public. Has a combined subject, name geographic index.

State Legislative Sourcebook
By: *Lynn Hellebust (Government Research Service);* Annual.
Describes legislative processes and structures of all 50 states, D.C., and Puerto Rico. Contains an extensive guide to state information resources, as well as pertinent addresses and phone numbers.

State Yellow Book
By: *Monitor Publishing Company;* Semi-annual.
Lists current addresses and phone numbers of over 30,000 officials in the executive, legislative and judicial branches of state government. Organized by state. Also provides brief state profiles.

Municipal/County Executive Directory
By: *Carroll Publishing Company;* 1992.
One of the most comprehensive guides to local governments. Lists over 50,000 elected and appointed officials at the county, city, village, township and municipal levels. Arranged geographically, subdivided by name of agency. Updated twice annually.

INFORMATION BROKERS

Information brokers look up information for a fee by using reference books, telephone research, or an online database accessed by a modem and personal computer. Brokers will deliver the information requested in a variety of forms, such as a bibliography of what has been written on a particular subject, abstracts of written articles or "full text" copies of articles. Fees depend on the amount of time and expense involved in finding and presenting the information requested.

Providers of fee-based information services can be found in the following directory:

Burwell Directory of Information Brokers
By: *Burwell Enterprises;* 1992.
A comprehensive international directory of information brokers, researchers and free-lance librarians. Areas of specialty and fees are listed.

Full service brokers will gather the requested information, distill it, synthesize it, organize it, manage it, package it, and deliver it, in an efficient and cost-effective manner. Several examples of these brokers (as can be found in the *Burwell Directory*) are as follows:

Aubergine Information Services
1945 San Antonio Avenue
Berkeley, CA 94707
415/527-9064
FAX: 415/527-5770

Information Brokers of Colorado
2888 Bluff Street, Suite 152
Boulder, CO 80301
303/449-8896

The Information Specialists, Inc.
2490 Lee Boulevard
Cleveland, OH 44118
216/321-7500
FAX: 216/321-7683

Research on Demand, Inc.
2030 Addison Street, Suite 600
Berkeley, CA 94704
800/227-0750
In CA: 415/841-1145
FAX: 415/841-6311

The *Association of Independent Information Professionals* has become recognized within the information industry as the voice of the independent information professional. AIIP has over 300 members, publishes a quarterly newsletter, and has developed a standardized code of business ethics.

QUICK REFERENCE GUIDE TO BUSINESS INFORMATION POWER SOURCES

FAST TRACK INFORMATION GATHERING

When time is critically short, and you have no idea where to begin your data search, the following sources tend to be the most productive and easiest to use for finding information on almost any business topic.

Associations -- One of the single most valuable resources on any topic. Seek out and contact appropriate associations for current information and referrals. Source:

Encyclopedia of Associations
By: *Gale Research, Inc.*

Federal Government -- Locate appropriate department/agency to find relevant data, publications and services. Sources:

Monthly Catalog of U.S. Government Publications
By: *U.S. Government Printing Office (GPO)*

United States Government Manual
By: *U.S. General Services Administration*

Washington Information Directory
By: *Congressional Quarterly, Inc.*

Journal/Magazine/Newspaper Articles -- Utilize your library's reference section to look up your topic in both the traditional and CD-Rom/Online indexes. Sources:

Business Periodicals Index
Reader's Guide to Periodical Literature
New York Times Index
Predicast's Funk & Scott Index
Wall Street Journal Index
ABI/Inform and/or *Infotrac*
NEXIS/LEXIS

Experts -- Speak to at least three to five experts in the field being researched. This will yield answers to questions and also referrals to other sources. Experts include:

Authors of books
Staff writers and editors of periodicals
Government officials
Company executives
Convention Speakers
Consultants
Experts cited in news articles
Association staff members

BASIC BUSINESS INFORMATION POWER SOURCES

Information on some of the more common business subjects can be found quickly by checking the following sources:

Industry Information

- Brokerage Houses/Stock Analysts
  (e.g. Merrill Lynch, Paine Webber, etc.)
- Trade Associations
  (e.g. American Marketing Association)
- U.S. Department of Commerce
  (e.g. International Trade Administration, International Trade Commission, Federal Trade Commission and U.S. Industrial Outlook)
- Washington Legislative Information
  (e.g. Congressional Committee Hearings)
- Market Research Reports
  (e.g. Findex, FIND/SVP Studies)

Company Information

- Annual Reports
- Business Indexes
  (e.g. Business Periodicals Index, NY Times Index, Predicasts F&S Index, Wall Street Journal Index)

- Business Directories
  (e.g. Dun & Bradstreet Million Dollar Directory, Standard & Poor's Register and Ward's Business Directory)
- "Everybody's Business"
  (Harper & Row)
- SEC--Securities and Exchange Commission *(e.g. 10K Reports)*
- Chamber of Commerce
  (Business & Industry Directory)
- Better Business Bureau
  (performance records/investigations)
- Local Government
  (City Hall, County Clerk's Office)
- Local Media
  (business journals, e.g. Greater Cincinnati Business Record, Crain's [city] Business)

Product/Service Information

- Names/Trademarks
  (Trade Names Dictionary, Brands and Their Companies, Thomas Register, Trademark Register, Compu-Mark Directory of U.S. Trademarks)
- Trends
  (Advertising Age, Marketing News, Official Gazette of the U.S. Patent & Trademark Office)

Economic Statistics

- Bureau of the Census
  (e.g. County Business Patterns, County and City Data Book, Statistical Abstract of the United States, Census of Retail, Service and Wholesale Trades)
- Bureau of Economic Analysis
  (e.g. Survey of Current Business and Business Conditions Digest)
- Bureau of Labor Statistics
  (BLS News)
- Federal Reserve Board
  (Bulletins and other publications on banking, business conditions, money, interest rates, wages and prices)
- Internal Revenue Service
  (Statistics of Income Bulletin)

- United Nations
  (World Economic Survey, U.N. Monthly Bulletin of Statistics, The Demographic Yearbook)

Market and Consumer Information

- Demographics
  (1990 U.S. Census of Population & Housing, County and City Data Book, Consumer USA, Data Map, Surveys of Consumers)
- Trends
  (American Demographics, Lifestyle Market Analyst, Market Share Reporter, Gallop Poll Monthly)

Investment Information

- Standard & Poor's
  (The Outlook)
- New York Stock Exchange
  (Investor's Investment Kit)
- National Association of Securities Dealers
  (NASDAQ Fact Book and the Guide to Information and Services)
- Securities and Exchange Commission
  (What Every Investor Should Know)
- Dow Jones
  (The Wall Street Journal, The Dow Jones-Irwin Business and Investment Almanac)

Entrepreneurship

- Small Business Administration
  (Business Plan for Small Service Firms, Researching Your Market)
- National Technical Information Service
  (The Directory of Federal and State Business Assistance)
- U.S. Patent and Trademark Office
  (Basic Facts About Patents and Trademarks)
- Mailing List Companies
  (Yellow Pages: "Mailing Lists")
- Handbooks
  (Small Business Sourcebook, Macmillan Small Business Handbook)

International Information

- Commerce Department, Export Promotion Service
  (Catalog of Market Research Reports)
- Commerce Department, International Trade Administration
  (e.g. Overseas Business Report, Export Counseling Center)
- Commerce Department, Office of European Community Affairs
  (Single Internal Market: 1992 Information Service)
- Country Consulates and Embassies
  (Major U.S. cities)

Expert Information

- Government
  (U.S. Government Manual, Federal Executive Directory, State Data and Database Finder)
- General Business
  (Encyclopedia of Associations, Consultants & Consulting Organizations Directory, The Burwell Directory of Information Brokers, World Chamber of Commerce Directory)

"Information is a commodity that can be bought <u>and</u> sold."

- Cassandra Geneson,
Information Brokers of Colorado

INDEX

B

C

D

E

F

G

H

I

M

N

Q

V

W

Notes

Notes

INFORMATION PROJECT WORKSHEET

This worksheet is designed to assist you in beginning your search for business information on a specific topic.

Subject to Research: **(Major topic and sub-topics covered)**

1.

a.
b.
c.
d.

Libraries to Consult: **(Public, university, corporate, other)**

1.
2.
3.
4.
5.

Associations to Consult: **(Professional and trade)**

1.
2.
3.
4.
5.

Government Agencies to Consult: **(Federal, state, local)**

1.
2.
3.
4.
5.

Indexes and Databases to Consult: **(Printed and electronic)**

1.
2.
3.
4.
5.

Directories to Consult: **(Geographic, trade, special purpose)**

1.
2.
3.
4.
5.

Books, Documents, Statistical and Special Reports to Consult: **(Dictionaries, handbooks, manuals, census and other data reports)**

1.
2.
3.
4.
5.

Periodical Publications to Consult: **(Journals, magazines, newspapers, newsletters)**

1.
2.
3.
4.
5.

Experts to Consult: **(Government, business, academic, information brokers)**

1.
2.
3.
4.
5.

Other Sources to Consult:

1.
2.
3.
4.
5.

INFORMATION PROJECT WORKSHEET

This worksheet is designed to assist you in beginning your search for business information on a specific topic.

Subject to Research: **(Major topic and sub-topics covered)**

1.
    a.
    b.
    c.
    d.

Libraries to Consult: **(Public, university, corporate, other)**

1.
2.
3.
4.
5.

Associations to Consult: **(Professional and trade)**

1.
2.
3.
4.
5.

Government Agencies to Consult: **(Federal, state, local)**

1.
2.
3.
4.
5.

Indexes and Databases to Consult: **(Printed and electronic)**

1.
2.
3.
4.
5.

Directories to Consult: **(Geographic, trade, special purpose)**

1.
2.
3.
4.
5.

Books, Documents, Statistical and Special Reports to Consult: **(Dictionaries, handbooks, manuals, census and other data reports)**

1.
2.
3.
4.
5.

Periodical Publications to Consult: **(Journals, magazines, newspapers, newsletters)**

1.
2.
3.
4.
5.

Experts to Consult: **(Government, business, academic, information brokers)**

1.
2.
3.
4.
5.

Other Sources to Consult:

1.
2.
3.
4.
5.

Notes

ORDER FORM

Did you borrow this book from a friend or the library and now you'd like a copy of your own? Would you like to purchase additional copies for your department or colleagues?

For additional copies of . . .

THE DESKTOP
BUSINESS INTELLIGENCE
SOURCEBOOK

Send **$16.95**
Plus **$3.00** Shipping and Handling
Ohio residents add 6% Sales Tax **($1.02)**
Total Payment Enclosed
$__________

SHIP TO: (Please print clearly)

Mr./Ms.:

Company:

Address:

City/State/ZIP:

Telephone: ( )

Send this form and your payment (check or money order) to:

Hyde Park Marketing Group
Hyde Park P.O. Box 8804
Cincinnati, Ohio 45208

Please allow 2-3 weeks for delivery. Quantity discounts are available.
Please write to us for additional information.

ORDER TODAY !